PEOPLE ARE TALKING ...

Rick Frishman is one of only ten people who understand and have mastered the book publishing process—I have counseled with him, listened to him, and watched the books he promoted turn to gold. If you're looking for someone to take your book to the promised land, I promise that Rick Frishman is the rocket ship that will take you there.

—Jeffrey Gitomer, *King, Buy Gitomer, Inc.*

Judith Briles should be used by anyone in the process of writing or publishing a book. As a first time author, my learning curve was quite steep. Judith supported me every step of the process. She went beyond her original job description, always making sure all my needs were met. Her integrity was exemplary. Not only did we collaborate and complete my book, she then led me through the publishing aspects and now the marketing. I am truly grateful for Judith and her gifts, insights and knowledge. My book would not have happened without her! I highly recommend.

—Lynn Hellerstein, author of *See It. Say It. Do It!*

John Kremer is *Staggering*. No one tells the author these things—not the publisher, not the writer's rep. Just John Kremer.

—John Robert Marlow, screenwriter and author of *Nano*

Rick Frishman is one of the most well-connected people I know. He understands every aspect of author promotion and is able to deliver exactly what the individual project requires. His strategic thinking skills, his deep understanding of what really delivers, and his collaborative and positive personal style make Rick and his team a perfect choice for publishers and authors alike. Highly recommended.

—Cindy Ratzlaff, V.P., Associate Publisher, *Rodale Books*

1

Judith Briles is a brilliant woman who can take an idea for a book and translate that idea into reality. She is enjoyable to work with. The books that come from her clients are always top quality. She has my highest recommendation.

—Eric Kampmann, President, *Midpoint Trade Books, Inc.*

John Kremer is the go-to guy for marketing books. Not only are Kremer's tips and resources excellent for promoting books, but you can use many of the techniques and strategies for promoting a variety of other goods and services. Highly recommended!"

— Joel Comm, author, *The Twitter Handbook*

Rick Frishman is my go-to guy for book publicity and marketing. I trust him deeply and he's earned his reputation as an expert, a creative confidante, and the best book publicist in the nation.

—Brendon Burchard, author, *Life's Golden Ticket*

Judith Briles is a tireless advocate for authors and independent publishing; the knowledge and skills that she contributes to each project allow authors to produce top quality work and results that exceed expectations. She has a gift for knowing how best to spotlight an author's strengths, and her vast network of connections and resources ensure that authors are working with top notch professionals in all aspects of the publishing process. Judith also has a strength in evaluating challenges authors are experiencing and developing solutions to keep the momentum and energy going in the right direction. Whether you are a new or veteran author, Judith's creativity and expertise will take you to the next level in producing a superior book.

—Kelly Johnson, Owner, *Cornerstone Virtual Assistance*

John Kremer's seminar was wonderful and, as he predicted, not the least bit redundant. This is the single best thing I've done as far as workshops, etc. Thank you for all your information and for being who you are. That really shines through.

— Meredith Boyd, *Healing Visions Press*

In less than four years Morgan James Publishing has gone from a start-up to a $10 million business and was ranked number 44 on Fast Company's "Fast 50" Companies for 2006. As Morgan James founder I was even named a Finalist in the Best Chairman category in The 2006 American Business Awards. Hailed as "the business world's own Oscars" by the New York Post (April 27, 2005), The American Business Awards are the only national, all-encompassing business awards program honoring great performances in the workplace. Our efficient business model, enabled by our partnership with **Rick Frishman**, makes our success possible. We would never be where we are today without him.

—David Hancock, Founder, *Morgan James Publishing Company*

John Kremer is a boon on the planet. If I didn't have his book, newsletter, and website, I would be floundering right now.

—Kristin von Kreisler, author of *For Bea*

Rick Frishman is a genius when it comes to publicity. If you need someone to help you get into the media he's the go-to guy. And he's a great guy!

—Ellen Violette, eBook/Internet Coach, Author, and Copywriter, *Create A Splash. LLC, /The eBook Coach*

Judith Briles works dynamically and effectively to empower others in their quest for success in authoring and publishing. A highly successful author, speaker and publisher herself, she is unstoppable on behalf of her clients and colleagues. Where no apparent solution exists, she invents one. Judith doesn't do the work for you—she shows you how to do it and create the breakthrough you've been looking for.

—Mara Purl, Author and Publisher of *Haven Books*

John Kremer —He's smart, creative and clever, and he knows how to help you sell books.

—Jon Bard, Editor, *Children's Writing Update!*

Rick Frishman was "the go to guy" if you wanted to publicize your book or project two decades ago. Well, now he is an industry leader in the same category. Rick knows how to get eyes and ears on your project. He's still the go to guy.

—Jim Cathcart, President & Founder, *Cathcart Institute, Inc.*

When I run across people who are very serious about marketing their books and are teachable/coachable there is only one person for them to see. **Judith Briles** has gifts, experiences and knowledge of the book publishing/marketing is second to none. She can save her clients time, money and frustrations, but even more significant is the final product will be so different than what was brought her. She is amazing. We are raving fans of her.

—Dave Block and Victoria Munro, Co-Founders of *Make-it-fly.com*

John Kremer has helped a lot of us in the book industry. BookMarket. com is a very wonderfully resourceful tool for anyone who is an author, publisher, printer, book publicist, book promoter, or seller. He's done an excellent job compiling good, useful information that allows us all to grow exponentially.

—Kennetta Wainwright, CEO, *Redbone Book Management*

Rick Frishman is without a doubt one of the top book publicists in the country. Not only has he represented many best selling authors as the founder of Planned Television Arts, he has mentored hundreds of emerging authors and professional speakers including myself with his stellar workshops. Rick is truly a professional of the highest caliber and someone I am proud to call a colleague and friend. December 4, 2008

—Robert Stack, MCLC, APR, Fellow PRSA, Owner, *Fame Coach*

When I was introduced to **Judith Briles'** comprehensive business plan for authors, I felt that I had found the person and company that would take me from A to Z in the publishing world. Having written and published 26 books, Judith's knowledge of the writing and publishing field is superior. Her knack for turning writers into authors is amazing. Additionally, her abundant resources, which offer the highest caliber proficiency, are shared willingly. If you are somewhere between veteran and aspiring author, don't lose any time in meeting with this brilliant professional.

—Barb Tobias, author of *Tossed & Found*

John Kremer is truly a resource for writers and others in the book publishing and marketing business. I recommend him highly.

—Scott Lorenz, president, *Westwind Communications*

SHOW ME ABOUT:

BOOK PUBLISHING

*Survive and Thrive
in Today's
Literary Jungle*

JUDITH BRILES
RICK FRISHMAN
JOHN KREMER

New York

SHOW ME ABOUT:
BOOK PUBLISHING

Survive and Thrive in Today's Literary Jungle

by **JUDITH BRILES, RICK FRISHMAN, JOHN KREMER**

ISBN 978-1-60037-855-3 (paperback)

ISBN 978-1-60037-856-0 (ePub)

Library of Congress Control Number: 2010934171

Published by:

Morgan James Publishing
The Entrepreneurial Publisher
5 Penn Plaza, 23rd Floor
New York City, New York 10001
(212) 655-5470 Office
(516) 908-4496 Fax
www.MorganJamesPublishing.com

Cover Design by:
Rachel Lopez
Rachel@r2cdesign.com

Interior Design by:
Bonnie Bushman
bbushman@bresnan.net

Books may be purchased for sales promotion by contacting the publisher.

In an effort to support local communities, raise awareness and funds, Morgan James Publishing donates one percent of all book sales for the life of each book to Habitat for Humanity.
Get involved today, visit
www.HelpHabitatForHumanity.org.

Also Co-Authored by Rick Frishman:
Guerrilla Publicity
Guerrilla Marketing for Writers-2nd Edition
Networking Magic
Where's Your WOW
Author 101 Bestselling Book Publicity
Author 101 Bestselling Book Proposals
Author 101 Bestselling Nonfiction
Author 101 Bestselling Secrets from Top Agents
10 Clowns Don't Make a Circus
The Entrepreneurial Author

Also by John Kremer:
1001 Ways to Market Your Books
John Kremer's Self-Publishing Hall of Fame
Here's What You Should Know About Book Promotion
Choosing a Distributor

DEDICATION

To Authors, Publishers and Readers all over the world

and in other universes we have yet to reach.

TABLE OF CONTENTS

People Are Talking…   i

Dedication   xi

Acknowledgements   xv

Foreword – Dan Poynter   xvii

Introduction   1

1   Is There a Book in You?   9

2   What's What in Publishing Today … Yesterday is Yesterday   15

3   Money Talks … Do You Listen?   33

4   Your Publishing Team … Soloing Doesn't Work   47

5   To Shepherd, or Not to Shepherd? …
    That Shouldn't Be Your Question   63

6   Publishing Requires Editing … No Exceptions!   77

7   Front Matter, Back Matter and Other Matter   87

8   Book Covers Talk … Does Yours POP … or Snooze?   95

9   The Publishing Clock is Ticking …Practical Timelines   103

10 Pre-Publication Platforms …Sell Before You Print   119

11 Foreign Rights … Where Your Mailbox Finds a Friend   123

12　Rebounding When You Hit the Wall …
　　Everyone Gets Stuck Sometime　　　　　　　　　129

13　You Think You Are Done … You Are Not　　　　135

14　Mistakes to Avoid … Or Saving Money 101　　　141

15　Afterword　　　　　　　　　　　　　　　　151

16　Resources, Resources & More Resources　　　　153

　　Sneak Preview: Next in the *Show Me About* series …　　191

　　About the Authors　　　　　　　　　　　　199

ACKNOWLEDGEMENTS

No book is a solo act. The authors are always up front … we get to take the bows. Yet, it's all the players behind the scenes that really bring our words to you.

Each of us gives kudos to our co-authors as well as to the support from David Hancock and the Morgan James publishing team. The *Show Me About* series was seeded over breakfast one morning after a publishing conference. "What if we …." and the idea was off and running.

Rick also adds his thanks to his wife, Robbi, for her years of support and encouragement.

Judith tips her writing pen to husband John Maling who wore two hats—that of creating space for her to go into her binge mode of writing and as editor; Katherine Carol, her partner in *TheBookShepherd.com*; and her clients and publishing colleagues who said, "It's about time."

John wants to thank his wife Gail who puts up with a lot of his shenanigans while he plays at working hard. He also wants to thank his two dogs, Becky and Elsie, for taking him for walks every day to keep him in shape.

FOREWORD

For budding authors, there's often a time when they enter a book store, envisioning their forthcoming book amongst the myriad of books that are displayed. Each offering a solution, an idea or a fantastic adventure with the author's imagination as the guide. They see themselves receiving multiple offers from the New York publishing community and signing stacks of books—and then reality sets in.

It's a rare author who gets a New York deal, much less multiple offers. And I've always believed that book stores are a lousy place to sell books. Did you know that the average bookstore book signing sells six books? A mere, short stack. And that the average number of nonfiction books sold that was published by a New York house was fewer than 5,000 copies in 2009?

There's another way. And I believe, a better way. A way that I've shown and shouted about around the world. Since the initial publication of the *Self-Publishing Manual* in 1979 and the *Self-Publishing Manual Vol 2* in 2009, I've spoken to thousands upon thousands of beginning and established authors globally. Each has something in common: 1) to write a book, or in some cases, another book; 2) to find the best way to get it published and 3) to be financially successful.

In *Show Me About Book Publishing*, Judith Briles, Rick Frishman and John Kremer have created a guide that is a welcome addition to the publishing world. All acclaimed authors of dozens of books, they've succeeded in both the traditional and self-published worlds. And when given their druthers, they would select the latter.

Why? Because they understand the business of publishing; how to create a book that will be in demand; how to market a published book for maximum return; and the extensive use of traditional and social media in doing so. And, they understand that when you bring all the puzzle pieces together, the author can achieve amazing returns—moneywise and professionally. A rare experience for most authors today.

Welcome to the continuing, exciting times in publishing.

Dan Poynter,
The Self-Publishing Manual

INTRODUCTION

Publishing your own book is work. It's not for everyone. Before you set out on the path, ask yourself a few questions. We've got the *Big14* that require you to look into the mirror and answer "yes" or "no." Let's start.

The Show Me About Book Publishing Quiz

1. Are you passionate about your topic, your book?

2. Is being in control important to you?

3. Is it important that your topic get published within the next 4 to 6 months?

4. Do you have the time to commit to your book project?

5. Do you want your covers to look a certain way?

6. Is it important to have a quality looking book?

7. Are you willing to make mistakes, and correct them?

8. Do you have the financial resources to support your book, and you?

9. Are you willing to learn from the pros and educate yourself?

10. Are you persistent?

11. Do you know who your buyer is?

12. Do you have a niche?

13. Do you want to make money?

14. Are you willing to learn about the business of publishing?

Any *yeses*? Lots of them? The greater the number you have, the more you should publish yourself … and the more likely you will be successful. Below are our thoughts for you to consider with each of the Big 14.

1. *Are you passionate about your topic, your book?*

   Your words are you. That's a huge investment in itself. You've got to love what you are creating. Really care for it. Do you? It's like the difference between your job and your work … a job is a job, hopefully it pays the bills. But work? It's part of your fabric, who you are. And when you love your work, passion enters the scene.

2. *Is being in control important to you?*

   If you want your book cover to look a certain way; the interiors to have a specific presentation style; the paper to look or feel a certain way; the fonts to be of a definite type; the editing to be done your way that allows feedback; and to make input into the marketing strategies, control is important. With traditional publishers, you become a royal pain in the tush. Others may not give you options as well.

3. *Is it important that your topic gets published within the next 4 to 6 months?*

   If your book needs to be available within the year, the odds are that it won't happen with a traditional publisher. Normally, a book is published approximately 18 months after a publisher signs the author.

4. *Do you have the time to commit to your book project?*

   Creating a successful book takes time—lots of it. It's not just the writing. It's the book production that takes time and then all the post production marketing, which can go on for many, many months. If you want to be successful, you've got to become myopic at times and prioritize in favor of your book.

5. *Do you want your covers to look a certain way?*

   We know of few authors from the traditional publishing world that are enamored with their book covers. Cover control is like a parent withholding the family car keys from a teenager. It's power—publishers, and their marketing departments, often have fixed ideas that are in cement when it comes to covers. We know, we've had our share that we sometimes wanted to put a brown wrapper on. When we started publishing our own books, we liked the covers. So should you.

6. *Is it important to have a quality looking book?*

One of our friends had a book published in 2009 with a major publisher and did a visual comparison with another book published with the same publisher in 1984. The difference was amazing. The quality of the paper in the new version was thinner—it displayed the ink print on the other side; the quality of the cover in the older book—it laid flat. The newer one was already morphing open. The book that was 25 years old was in better shape than the book hot off the press. If the quality of how your book looks, feels and holds up is important, traditional, as well as other publishing options, may not work for you.

7. *Are you willing to make mistakes, and correct them?*

Every author makes mistakes. Every author turned publisher makes them. Can you forgive yourself? Can you ID from where the error was generated? Can you self-correct and redirect yourself?

8. *Do you have the financial resources to support your book, and you?*

You have to decide whether you are a hobbyist or casual author publisher, or ready to dive in and publish-publish. As a hobbyist, you will go the print-on-demand (POD) route for minimal moneys ($500 to $1500). But, as a serious author-publisher, you must be ready to invest several thousand dollars. Editors, designers and printers all add up. However, if you are successful, you can make an excellent return. It all goes back to passion, time, commitment, strategy and marketing.

9. *Are you willing to learn from the pros and educate yourself?*

You need to develop publishing smarts. There are plenty of books and workshops out there to help you fast-forward your learning curve. The more you learn, the fewer mistakes you will make. We come across self and independent publishers every day who have kissed off thousands of dollars by failing to educate themselves. This project is part of the investment: becoming publishing smart and getting involved.

The classic books include :

Self-Publishing Manual by Dan Poynter

Self-Publishing Manual, Vol 2 by Dan Poynter

1001 Ways to Market Your Book by John Kremer

Guerrilla Publicity by Jay Conrad Levinson , Rick Frishman and Jill Lublin

How to Make Real Money Selling Books by Brian Jud

Guerrilla Marketing for Writers by Jay Conrad Levinson, Rick Frishman, Michael Larsen and David Hancock

Networking Magic by Rick Frishman and Jill Lublin

Join groups such as:

IBPA (Independent Book Publishers Association at *www.IBPA-online.org* Author U at *www.AuthorU.org*.

Attend their conferences, Boot Camps and Author 101 University at *www.AuthorUniversity101.com* and *www.AuthorU.org*.

For marketing, John Kremer hits a homerun with his Ten Million Eyeballs online events at *www.TenMillionEyeballs.com*. Dan Poynter's newsletter, Publishing Poynters is also a must read at *www.ParaPublishing.com* as is Brian Jud's Book Marketing Matters at *www.BookMarketingWorks.com*.

The bottom line: don't jump in without understanding what the process is all about. Otherwise, you will kiss off a lot of money correcting mistakes before getting it right.

10. *Are you persistent?*

Every successful author and publisher has "persistent" as their middle name. You must become a promoter and sales agent for your book. That requires multiple follow-ups to any leads you have … and constantly getting new ones. It's drilling down to aggressively finding and then going to your buyer. Self and Independent publishing can get your book to the market three times faster than the traditional publisher. In this way, you get a quick start out of the gate; but it doesn't stop there—now, you've got to keep moving.

11. ***Do you know who your buyer is?***

The most common error we see authors-turned-publishers do is that they believe that their books are for the general masses. No, they are not. The most successful authors and publishers know who their buyer is—you may have a terrific idea for a romance series—but did you know that not all women like romance novels? And okay the ones that do may not like graphic sex scenes—they prefer just a hint? Or that some like the Jane Austen formula while others think it's bloody boring? Yes, women are the market, but which of the markets within the market?

12. ***Do you have a niche?***

We believe that the more you niche within the target segment, the greater your success can become. Judith published a book called *Woman to Woman: From Sabotage to Support* in the 80s. It was for the working woman—and there are lots of them. When she spoke for a community group of women in NY in the early 90s, several nurse executives heard her and encouraged her to focus on healthcare—lots of women still, just a narrower group than all working women. She did multiple studies, drilling down within the healthcare market and published another book. That was more than a decade ago. To date, three additional books have been published dealing with conflict resolution within the female dominated nursing workplace. Each book has been successful with multiple printings.

John has done the same thing within publishing. There are numerous books on marketing and sales—for everybody. His

1001 Ways to Market Your Book is one of the few "must haves" for authors and publishers alike. His niche.

The moral: If you drill down within a group—your group—write and publish for it. You can be the big fish. It's better to be the whale in the pond vs. the sardine in the ocean.

13. ***Do you want to make money?***

Traditional publishers pay 6 to 9 percent on trade paper books and anywhere from 10 to 15 percent on hardback books. Some pay on the retail sales price; most now pay on the net money received. It's not really a good deal unless you have a runaway best-seller. If you target and niche your markets, it's not uncommon to be able to sell at a 95 percent of the retail price with a worst case, 55 percent which is the wholesale discount. In publishing, number-crunching needs to be done. If you want to make money, independent publishing is your route; expect some zig-zags along the way. And, you need a plan—your marketing plan—to make your publishing a success.

14. *Are you willing to learn about the business of publishing*

Authors are creative; it takes plenty of imaginative juice to write a book. It's equally important once published to now direct that creative juice to the business side. As an independent publisher, you are now *running a business*. You are the decision maker for marketing plans, printing, fulfillment and inventory control. You can hire people to handle it for you, but you need to know what they are doing in the first place. If you don't, there will be trouble.

The self and independent publishing markets are growing substantially within the book world—sales are now in the mega billions. In gross revenues, traditional publishing still outsells the independent market, but their sales are on a decline. Because of the ability of the independent publisher to get a quality book published within a shorter period of time, opportunities abound—opportunities that traditional publishers can't respond to.

The purpose of ***Show Me About Book Publishing*** is to eliminate the mumbo-jumbo that small publishers run into and suffer from along with introducing a realistic and reasonable approach to publishing today.

Creating a book—and a publishing company—is a huge investment of your time ... and your money. HUGE. Our personal goal is for you to come away with a variety of ideas that will enhance your authorship and publishing journey and reduce the amount of money that you would normally spend to complete it.

With the three of us as your guides, you've got partners that have been there, done that.

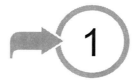

IS THERE A BOOK IN YOU?

Think of publishing as the world's largest shopping mall. The main anchor stores would include Random House, Simon & Schuster, McGraw-Hill, John Wiley & Sons, Harper (without the Collins) and Grand Central. Boutiques would be everywhere—large and small—Source Books, Adams Media, Scholastic and some are hybrids like Morgan James Publishing or small and plain vanilla such as Mile High Press and Open Horizons … an unbelievable menu to select from.

Different sections of the mall feature genres—romance, travel and cookbooks on the north wing; sci-fi, suspense, and fantasy on the east section; self-help and how-to, business, and psychology can be nestled in the west; and the south offers up a plethora of everything else you can imagine including a variety of stores that offer accessories and consulting services to all things publishing. Publishing generates over 25 billion in annual revenues.

Why do people publish a book? Why do authors write them? The reasons are numerous. One of the ways to enhance your status as *the expert* is to write a book. For others, it's their life's work. You could have had an epiphany of some sort; experienced an amazing event or feat; you may be bubbling over with ideas for children's books or the next murder mystery series.

Who knows how you got here … what you do know, is that you have heard the calling. Somewhere, in there, the Publishing Siren beckons to you. The Author. What book is in you?

For Judith, it happened one night. After dinner with a well known national columnist and author, he used/took some of her ideas in a column that he published, and was paid for. She was not. Her take away "aha": if she didn't start taking and using her own ideas, others would … and publish them. Her first book, *The Woman's Guide to Financial Savvy* was published by St. Martin's Press in 1981. That has led to 26 additional books and counting. Her journey has taken her from publishing with the big New York houses, the big agents, to creating her own imprint.

For Rick, it was an offshoot of his radio producing days with WOR in New York that led to the establishment of PTA—Planned Television Arts with Michael Levine. Rick became the creative brain behind the many best-selling media strategies for well-known authors like Wayne Dyer, Howard Stern, Arnold Palmer, the Duchess of York, Jack Canfield, Mark Victor Hansen and *The Notebook's* Nicholas Sparks. His first book, *Guerrilla Marketing for Writers*, was co-written with Jay Conrad Levinson, Michael Larsen and David Hancock. Rick is the first to admit that he's not a great writer … but he's a great partner. His books are all co-written; *Show Me About Book Publishing* his 12th.

For John, it was frustration that brought him to publishing his first book. He was desperately in search of a resource on book printers. There wasn't one, so he created *101 Ways to Print Your Book* in 1986. Today, his book, *1001 Ways to Market Your Book* is considered a "must have" by any author who is serious about selling books.

Each of us came to the authoring party from a different route. We heard the Publishing Siren … and we responded.

You, the author—your savvy words, stories or illustrations, your fantasies, your successes in working with specific industries, types of clients—provide case studies that may not include names, but gives someone looking for help hope that there is someone out there that understands their industry, situation and concerns. You've heard the Siren.

Does everyone have a book in them? No. But if you do, you must face the facts: there's competition for readership. The simple truth is that there are too many books being published today. And of them, there are too many books that are mediocre looking—from cover and interior layout design to being content poor. To survive—succeed— your book should look, and feel, good. A stand-out in the crowded book world.

Credentials Talk ... You've Got Them

People like to work with and get advice from people who they feel are successful. When potential clients have the opportunity to read about your philosophy, your strategies for specific situations, it's a huge door opener for future business. And a good reason to become an author. The biggest sellers are in to the "how-to" and business arenas.

What if you write for juveniles, romance, stovetop warriors or just kids? Credentials and writing/artistic skill carry a huge stick in the publishing arena.

Having a book, with your name as the author on it, adds a significant notch in the credibility game. It goes beyond just a business card; it becomes part of your guts and soul. There isn't a gathering of people where someone, in fact, many ones, will share that they feel that they have a book in them.

Smart Authors are Savvy Positioners

Look in the mirror. Authors ask questions, here's yours ...

- What separates you from other authors?
- What are you an expert in?
- Do you have work (or savings/investments) that generates more than enough cash flow to exceed your expenses, allowing you to write and market your book?
- Do you have repeat clients?

- Are you known as the "go to" person to solve a problem or to consult with for others?
- Or, do you feel/see that you are still in the pack and haven't broken out?
- Have you told anyone about what separates you from the pack?
- Have your written about it?
- Have you done any branding on yourself?
- Does the world know where, and how to find you … easily?
- Do you have a platform—one that you are easily recognized within?
- Do you have a website that immediately "tells" the visitor who you are, what your expertise is and how they can contact you?
- Would you like to create a book merely as a business card—one that you have available via your website and listing on Amazon or do you want to create a strategy to sell it?
- If your objective is to sell books—lots of them—do you have the platform to seed sales?
- Do you know the difference between traditional, self and independent publishing?
- Do you know what options you have to publish?
- Do you know what the options cost?
- Do you have the time to commit to writing a book?
- Do you have the time, and moxie, to commit to positioning and selling a book?

The Yin and Yang of Publishing

With books, the author has to tune into her message, listen to what she hears her "audience" say it needs/wants. She reflects, evaluates and connects with the core of what the book is about. Yin is all about emotion and with emotion, the passion for "why" this book—your book—will be created and birthed.

It's the yang, though, that will get it to happen. The author is challenged with a goal to expand the ideas and concepts that originally seeded the idea. The big stretch starts—what's new; what concepts and solutions have a twist to them that makes them unique to what has been published before. What can you turn on its head or tweak a commonly held belief? It's the new approach that gathers attention.

In the end, the author comes away with knowledge of the publishing process along with the tools to implement it.

Creating a book and using it as part of your marketing campaign enhances your positioning as *the Authority, the Expert.* Your credibility. And, a positioning factor in building your brand and your "business" as an author. To us, it doesn't matter what "your business" is—be it business, finance, sci-fi, kids, mystery or even a bit of romance. What we want you to think, to realize, is that publishing isn't a lark—being an author is an honor and a very legit business to be in. We will show you how.

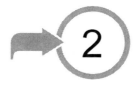

WHAT'S WHAT IN PUBLISHING TODAY ... YESTERDAY IS YESTERDAY

Once upon a time, there were two types of publishing. The first was traditional where an author had an idea, created a proposal or manuscript, acquired an agent to represent him and sold it to a publisher. Preferably, a New York publisher. The other was one that was looked at with disdain and pooh-poohed ... the vanity press. Traditional authors were viewed as snobs by the vanity press crowd ... and envied.

Authors went the vanity press route as a publishing format of the last resort. They couldn't "sell" their book idea to New York and had decided to hook up with a vanity publisher, selling a few copies at a time. Vanity presses were usually small shops that the author would pay to publish his book. Under the vanity press umbrella was self-publishing, the do-it-yourself model. Vanity and self-published meant the same thing—it was where the rejects went.

If you took the vanity press route, any success your book would have would be exclusively in your ballpark. Vanity publishers did nothing to promote your book—you were strictly on your own. The number of copies printed of your book would be the number that you ordered printed, paying up front for them. The quality of the book was, well, so-so. Mass distribution, marketing or PR were non-existent. And forget about making any money to seed your retirement.

An offer from a traditional publisher was different. The author usually got thousands of books into print, a real media release created by the publisher's publicity department—one that was sent out to the media and bookstores—and an announcement, including a copy of the cover and a description of your book. It was placed in the publisher's catalog that reps took around to bookstores and used to pitch for orders. To add icing to the cake, it was not uncommon for the author to get a multi-city book tour to boot. Wahoo! The author was in the big leagues! Hot.

Ahhh, times have changed. Dramatically. That was the old days—pre 2000. With the Internet and today's technology, traditional publishers are being turned on their heads and vanity presses have morphed into new critters. Mega thousands of authors are choosing to bypass the traditional method that had been so coveted by the majority of authors just a few years ago. Even authors who have made major best-seller lists, such as the *New York Times*, are now positioning themselves outside of the "norm"—they are moving into self and independent publishing.

Many of the major publishers are struggling. During 2008 and 2009, major publishing houses announce the elimination of much loved imprints; the layoffs of highly respected editors; even the decision to not buy new titles for the forthcoming season.

Advances to authors dwindled significantly and the number of new books contracted for, plummeted. In many cases, authors got little to no advances and are told that being "published" by a major publisher is the prestige payment in lieu of!

As the decade turns, R.R. Bowker, the book industry's keeper of stats, reported that over 1,000,000 books were published in 2009—new books, revised books, university press books, mainstream books, eBooks, traditionally published books, small press books, vanity press, self and independent books. Books, books and more books. The number grows daily.

Publishers included the well known imprints of Random House and Simon & Schuster (the big boys); to the small and independent presses that you might have heard of like Open Horizons (John's imprint); to the self-published and vanity-type presses-(i.e., iUniverse, LuLu, AuthorHouse). Formats include the traditional paper book to the cyber-space delivered eBook. There's something for everyone.

 In 2008, it was reported that for the first time, the self and independent publishers were actually out-producing the traditional New York type of publisher. In 2009, the numbers soared even higher.

Amazon's Kindle rekindled the eBook genre that was birthed, and fizzled, in the 90's. At the industry's huge trade show, Book Expo of America, CEO Jeff Bezos reported to a packed room in June of 2008 that eBook sales were actually fueling huge sales for Amazon's paper books. Thousands of the eBook buyers wanted the hard copy after reading the eBook version! And, Amazon was partnering with major publishers to include more of their books in the Kindle book format.

The much anticipated Apple Computer's entre into the eBook market could be a huge push for eBook sales, and possibly the death knell for Kindle. Why?—Kindle does a so-so job with graphics and tables—something that Apple excels in. Time will tell.

Publishing—the New York version—has been around for 75 plus years. Also known as the Depression Model, here's what it looks like:

- Books are sold on consignment;
- If the bookstore sells them, the publishing house gets paid money;
- If the bookstore doesn't, all it has to do is return the unsold books;
- It's OK to keep the consignment inventory for several months before the bookstore decides if it wants to return them for credit; and

- If the bookstore pays the publishing house for any books sold, the author *may* eventually get a royalty, usually three to six months *after* the sale was made.

Archaic? You bet. And still, the vast majority of New York houses embrace the model; and authors scramble to enter into these medieval contracts for the "prestige" of being "under contract."

Authors literally give their rights and souls away for the "honor" of being published by a "real" publisher. Here's the truth: it's very, very difficult to get a deal that has any bones to it today. For every Tim Ferris breakout (*The Four-Hour Work Week*), there are 10,000 wannabes that have books fall on their written faces. Unless you, dear author, land in the top five percent, your big time publishing experience will most likely be one big time let down, sucking wind. Deals are hard to come by; every major publisher is downsizing and editors are downright fearful.

We suggest you breathe deeply and consider your options.

The New Big Four

Is there hope? Is there an out? Could there be a better way to get published? Absolutely, and we are here to show you why and how.

More and more authors are opting to go solo, creating their own publishing houses. Why—simply this: It's about *quality*; it's about *timing*; it's about *control*; and it's about *money*.

The quality of the books published by mainstream publishers has changed. Paper is thinner; interior designs are iffy; and editing is so-so. The reality is, today's savvy author can create a better product, make money, and have a good time in the process. And not gasp for air.

Authors want input on how their books look and what they say. With a traditional publisher, cherished titles morph; and decisions about how the book will "look" are made without the authors input or OK. Control flies out the window.

Messages and timing are always critical—unless a book has been "fast-tracked" by a publishing house … meaning it's being pushed to get out within a few months—expect a book to be published 18 months after it's accepted by the publisher. Eighteen months is a long time—when you want your message out now. Your hot idea could be obsolete by the time your printed word appears. Here today, gone tomorrow.

Finally, the money issue can be shocking. Traditional publishers pay between 10 and 15 percent royalties on the net or retail price of the book—it's all in the contract—contracts after the year 2000, leaned toward the net number. Why is that important? Simply this—the average non-fiction book sells less than 6,500 copies. At the end of 2009, reports coming from New York indicated that overall sales for mid-list books (not the Jim Collins, Tim Ferris type of books) were in the 3,000 to 4,000 range. This won't seed your retirement nest egg.

Indeed. The old days, are, well, old. Dinosaurian. The new model of author, as publisher, has birthed. And we think it's a very, very good thing.

Going Solo as an Initial Strategy

And, in some cases, going solo is part of an overall strategy to go big. What do we mean? Simply this: authors are publishing their own books with all the bells, whistles and trappings that a New York house does; creating sales via their platforms and crowds that know and love them; and then doing a pitch to New York. "Look at me. I've sold thousands … and you need me, more that I need you!"

Does New York need the proven author—one that can move and sell books? More than ever. But New York is afraid. The old model isn't working. Truth be told, most editors who acquire books aren't so clever. They may get their latest ideas from an article they read in a magazine or see something on TV. Or, the Internet. Without the blog world, would the best selling *Julie and Julia* have found its way to the bookshelf?

With the normal lag time of 18 months in publishing a book, the author who gets attention is the one who walks in with the book, the cover, an attractive interior design, the appropriate endorsements and an audience that has already stated via sales that there is a demand. In fact, it's common for publishers' representatives to scout the local best-seller lists of book stores to search for "indie" publishers and approach them.

Judith's book, *The Confidence Factor*, was on the best-seller list for many months at one of the nation's premiere independent book stores, The Tattered Cover in Denver, Colorado. She was approached by several publishers to "sell" the book to them. In the end, she turned down the offers to "re-publish" the book under their imprint. Why?—she didn't need, or want it. Judith could make far more money doing what she was doing in the way that she was promoting and selling it. Maintaining control of the quality of the book that would be produced was the deal-breaker for her.

The Players

There are seven major publishing formats authors opt for, knowing that new ones will be birthed as time evolves: *Traditional, Independent, Self, Subsidy, Packager, POD* (print-on-demand) and *eBook*. POD is also used in the subsidy area, standing for a publish-on-demand format. Each has merits and deficiencies.

Traditional Publishers

Most think of New York when it comes to traditional publishing—university presses come under this umbrella as well as a slew of publishers in other states. They acquire manuscripts; often work with agents and pay royalties. If your book is successful, it could be a great relationship. If your book doesn't "stick," meaning that it doesn't develop a following within six weeks or so, you and your book will most likely be tossed under the bus.

The publishers in this category can be huge: such as Simon & Schuster, Random House, Grand Central (formally Warner Books), and McGraw Hill; a university press like University of New Mexico Press, Harvard University Press and Chicago University Press; or an intermediate/smaller house, such as Source Books or Adams Media. Many traditional publishers have multiple imprints that are usually specialty publishers.

What sets them apart is that they pay royalties to their authors based on a percentage of book sales. Some pay advances—they can arrange from a few thousand to millions of dollars, depending on topic, author, the author's platform, celebrity, the negotiating skills of the agent, and sometimes even the whim of the publisher.

Many believe that they have to be published by a name publisher. This is a myth. How many times do you buy a book because of the publisher vs. the topic/content and/or author? Never is the most likely response.

The advantages that come with an affiliation with a traditional publisher include the simple fact that they front all the production costs to get it to market and you don't. The author doesn't have to worry about finding cover and interior designers, editors, creating media releases, wholesalers and distributors. Obtaining ISBN numbers, making announcements in Books in Print, copyright registration and all the components of getting your book from your original manuscript to print are taken care of. Some publishers create a book tour and they send your books to all the key reviewers. For some authors, being with a publisher is important to their image. For them, it's prestige. We call it the snob factor.

If your book clicks and sells well, it usually means that your publisher will offer more money for your next book and/or you will be courted by other publishers to come to them. For more money.

The disadvantages match all the advantages in number and add a few more nuggets to the mix. Yes, you don't have to worry about editors—assuming your editor is in synch with you. ISBNs, Library of Congress numbers, getting listed in Books in Print, but our joint experience has shown that too, too many authors aren't happy campers.

More authors than not, moan and groan about how much they dislike their covers; the interior design is so-so; the media release really doesn't have the "pop" it should; there are no books in the bookstores; the marketing/PR department has dozens of their books that they are pitching at the same time as yours; and the length of time to get your manuscript published can range from 15 to 24 months after submission.

Then there's the money. Publishers pay royalties twice a year based on a six-month timeframe (January-June and July-December) and delay the payment for three months for each period (to September and March). Normally, moneys—your earned royalties—are held back as a reserve in case book stores send books back.

Should you be publishing traditionally? Yes, if:

- You get offered huge money;
- You are a star and publishers will be mesmerized by your persona;
- You are a bit of a snob and your ego needs it—it's more important for you to be connected with a "name" publishing house;
- You just want to write the book and you want someone else to take care of everything else;
- You still have to work your tush off (surprise—publishers do very little for their stable of authors today and many expect their authors to use a major portion of the advance, if any, to underwrite marketing and PR that the author contracts for on his own); and
- You commit to focusing a great deal of your advance on marketing efforts.

If you sign with a publisher, we strongly advise you to make sure you understand how you can terminate your contract if the relationship goes south or ends. Pay attention to the Reversion of Rights clause. Besides having an agent, it's publishing smart to invest a few hours of your time with an attorney who understands publishing contracts.

Self-Publishers

From the vanity presentation that could never find its way to a shelf in a bookstore (most likely a LuLu type of book) to a slick presentation that a buyer at first glance assumes is from a traditional publisher, the self and independently published books from small presses have prospered.

Self-publishers range from those who only envision selling a few books to those who sell thousands of them. Many *New York Times* bestsellers began their publishing journeys via the self-publishing route. The usual reason is that they couldn't get a publisher to pick it up and/ or get an agent to become their champion, thus never getting it to a publisher's doorstep.

Self-publishing's Hall of Fame includes mega seller John Grisham. His first book, *A Time to Kill*, started out published by the author after multiple rejection notices and was later sold to Fleming H. Revell for a few thousand dollars. Revell in turn sold it for over a million dollars for much needed cash.

Management guru Tom Peters rolled out *In Search of Excellence* in self-published format before it was bought by New York; and Ken Blanchard started his *One-Minute* series from the kitchen table as did *What Color is Your Parachute?* author, Richard Nelson Bolles. Betty J. Eadie birthed *Embraced by the Light* on the self-publishing route along with Sandra Haldeman Martz with her *When I Am an Old Woman, I Shall Wear Purple* and Richard Evans with his *The Christmas Box.*

Then, there are a couple of reference gems that started the self-publishing route. Consider *Robert's Rules of Order* by Henry Martyn Robert and the all-time classic, *The Elements of Style*, by William Strunk, Jr. and EB White. To date, over 10 million copies of those tomes have been sold.

All were rejected by traditional publishing the first go around. The authors had their vision and did it themselves. By the time New York came to the party, the checks written were quite hefty.

There is a difference between self-publishing and independent publishing. Most people put the two in the same pot. Don't. Self-publishing is certainly on your own. So is independent. Within the self-publishing category is what we call the "hobbyist" or "casual" publisher. Making money isn't the key factor. Just having a book is. Most self-published books look, well, self-published. Money isn't dedicated to quality, although the content can be quite good. If you plan on selling less than 300 copies, this is a reasonable route to take.

Consider self-publishing if:

- You really plan on doing just one book;
- You plan printing a limited number of copies;
- Your primary goal is not to make money;
- You consider publishing an avocation, not a vocation;
- You want to do a "test" to see if there are any buyers out there; or
- You didn't know there is any other way and no one talked to you about creating your own publishing imprint.

Independent Publishers

All the above for Self Publishing holds here with the exception that being a single book author isn't a likely option. The majority of independent Publishers have a line of books. Or they create a book that hits, often creating by-products or spin-offs based around the book. An independent can be created by one author, himself; by authors other than the publisher; or they can be a combo—the publisher/author and other authors. And one of their goals is to be profitable. They view themselves as a business.

Small presses come under the independent umbrella. A good independent has its own imprint name, sets out to make money, and puts the time, energy and money into creating a quality product. It's not uncommon to see many small presses actually create a better looking product—the book—than New York puts out. Independents can access the same cover artists, interior designers and printers that a traditional publishing house does. They view publishing as a business, not a hobby.

Is there Independent Publishing in you? Yes, if:

- You want to be financially successful in publishing;
- You are willing to make a financial commitment to building your success;

- You are willing to learn about publishing;
- You are willing to work your tush off; and
- You are not a publishing snob.

Subsidy or Pay-to-Publish Publishers

Also known as pay-to-publish, there are several companies that take up-front money to publish your book. Subsidy publishers throw into the package, interior and cover design (don't expect miracles—most will use their formula templates). The author then gets to buy the book at a pre-set cost for resale. Most subsidy type of publishing uses a POD format—print-on-demand—for book ordering. You can buy one copy for resale or hundreds. The entry fee is usually less than $1,000 to enter into a contract … but, and it's a big but, the cost can be quite extensive per book unit; author/publisher discounting deals are pro-publisher, always; and getting out of a contract if things are not going well, can be difficult, if not impossible.

Should you subsidize someone else's publishing venture? Maybe, if:

- They offer something with the "package" that you would have to pay additional moneys for;
- If you aren't fussy about how your book looks and feels;
- If being in control isn't important to you; or
- If, after you crunch the cost of publishing, and understand clearly what you will get from the publisher, you decide that it's still worth it to you.

Book Packagers

Using a "putting it together" formula, an author will pay a lump sum—usually hefty—to a packager to edit (sometimes minimal, sometimes extensive); get the designer for the cover and interior; get print bids; and maybe help with a media release or other items within the package. When the process is all done, you have a book in print and are "published." Some packagers actually will put the book together and even take it to a mainstream publisher to try to publish.

Would a book packager make sense? Yes, if:

- You are so clueless, and you want someone else to do everything for you;
- Money isn't an issue, you've got plenty of it; or
- You really want someone there calling the shots and making the decisions.

POD (print-on-demand)

PODs became the answer to the vanity press crowd. It's also known as a short-run book. POD is a type of printing. Most self-publishers use a POD format. One book, a dozen, even a hundred at a time. POD costs more per unit than a book that is done in an offset print run and/or a higher volume of copies. Cost per book will depend upon the printer; whether the book is trade paper or hardback; use of color and the number of copies printed at a time.

Does a POD ever make sense? Sure, here's a few ways:

- If you want to do a short run to "test" your book—is there a market for it? There are printers who are strictly PODs, not publishers, and can do the print run—you still front the editing, designing and anything else you need to create the book. You also need to get the ISBN;
- You want to do a "test" run to get lots of copies out in readers hands to look for those typos that always manage to crop up, even after three different editors have looked at it;
- You really do have a limited run of books desired;
- You don't expect to sell more than 300 books; or
- Your book has run its course and you want to still have it available to the public.

If an author's goal is to get their books into a bookstore, POD isn't the option. Nor, if the goal is to sell lots of copies, is POD the option to take. The cost per unit is too high after all the discounting cuts are taken.

In fact, it may cost the author more to get the book sold via the bookstore than what he actually receives!

> The wife of one of the longest sitting federal Judges wanted to surprise her husband one Christmas. He had penned his experiences of life and on the bench for his personal records. She had them edited, designed the cover herself using personal photos, and used a POD publisher to have 100 copies ready for family and close friends on Christmas Eve. All of us in on the "secret" were very excited and looked forward to having his memoir in hand.
>
> It wasn't all smooth. The publisher had a so-so person on his staff oversee the project and several mistakes were made. When there had been plenty of time to get the project done per the publisher's stated timeframe, the screw-ups on its side gummed up the works. She had to pay extra fees to get her precious copies delivered on Christmas Eve, with many of them damaged from the very expensive overnight delivery to her.
>
> In the end, the family was thrilled, the Judge was surprised and honored and she was frazzled.

ePublishers

eBooks were hot in the 90s and almost died. The public wasn't ready. Quality was so-so and the listed price per book was fairly cheap. That has changed. With new formats, advancements in eReaders and the public being more accepting of reading copy from the computer and hand-helds, eBooks have rebirthed. The good news is that the retail price per unit has increased as well. It's not uncommon to see the eBook and the trade publication sell at comparable prices.

Is there an eBook for you? Possibly, if:

- You currently have a book;
- You are going to publish a book;
- You want to do a mini release of your forthcoming book; or

- You want to keep your book available when it's not in a paper format.

eBooks don't represent a huge segment of the book buying population, but guaranteed, it's growing. Amazon's Kindle renewed the public's interest. With the entry of Apple's iPad in 2010, it will only accelerate. With Apple in the mix, anything is possible, pay attention to what it continues to introduce. We feel it will morph the publishing game.

As the toddler in publishing, the eWorld has lots of players—and no real standard formats. Time will sort that out. The readers aren't cheap—in 2010, they ranged from $139 to $2,000. The odds are, as with all electronics, prices will begin to drop dramatically.

ePublishing will explode into another dimension that is the twinkle in many of a designer's eye at this writing. Some will fizzle and some will pop. Our opinion is that it doesn't make business sense to not have your books available in this format.

Eliminating Publishing Skulduggery

Before you enter into any contract, do some checking. There are several author and publisher friendly sites:

- The Author's Guild, *www.AuthorsGuild.org*, is one resource;
- Another was created by the Science Fiction and Fantasy Writers of America, *www.SFWA.org/beware*;
- Whispers and Warnings can be found at *www.WritersWeekely. com*; and
- Don't forget just Googling a publisher, vendor or supplier's name and put "complaints," "scams," "warning," or "problems" after the name. If there are alerts and grumblings, they will surface.

Book Coaching Eases the Journey

Coaches traditionally ask their clients questions as they work with them, often expecting them to seek the answers and solutions prior to the next coaching session. Shepherds are interactive from day one. They start putting together the game plan that gets the author writing and/or on the path to publishing his book.

As book coaches, they need answers and the contacts to supply solutions when appropriate. Oh, there will be questions, plenty of them, that the coach will be using, and repeating, throughout the process. But, when the author/publisher needs input, now is the best time. The next session may be too distant as with a traditional coach. That's where the shepherding hat kicks in.

An effective Book Shepherd and coach must have roots—deep ones—in the book arena. A hands-on, in-the-trenches experience.

As we wrote this, Judith was coaching a turnaround specialist in the creation of his first book. He is engaged by a company to quickly access a situation and advise as to whether it—the company—should be "fixed" or "dumped." Whichever option is chosen, he then steps in as an interim COO to save or bury it.

In the process of our first meeting, he was asked a series of questions that expanded his vision of what he really wanted to do with his skills and how the book would be the springboard to move him into international recognition.

He, initially, wanted a book to use as a business/calling card. Nothing more, nothing less. Two hours later, he had a totally different vision. A calling card was part of it, but there was so much more.

All derived from the questions asked, with the first being, "What was his objective in being in her offices today?"

From that, he dominoed the book as a business card idea to building an international consulting firm that had him speaking for corporations, primarily CEOs, and the creation of a variety of tools he could publish. His turn-around tools are the buzz within his profession.

The next step was the sequencing, the process and the how-tos to pull it off. The yang along with the yin.

The Publishing Siren

For the past year, Judith has said she would create the BSB—the Book Screw-up Barometer … or maybe call it the Book Screwed Barometer. On the low side, the amount of money that was quickly determined to be kissed-off per author among those of her clients seeking rescue was a few thousand dollars. The one that got the prize, though, was over $40,000.

Authors who hear the Siren often jump in too soon. They are excited— they want to get it done, *now*. They figure that they can find out all they need by reading a book or two or what can be gleaned from articles from the Internet. Wrong, wrong, wrong. Causes of failure can include one or more of the following:

- Not doing your pre-work
- Not creating a plan
- Not using a professional editor
- Not knowing that your manuscript needs professional help
- Not knowing that there are different editors for different jobs
- Not using the right cover and interior designer
- Not creating true marketing copy for the back cover
- Not engaging the right printer
- Not becoming the expert
- Not having a written plan
- Not doing targeted media/PR marketing
- Not staying visible
- Not treating authorship and publishing as a business
- Not understanding the financials
- Not cutting-off people who don't work with and for you
- Not being loyal to your book and your vision
- Not seeking the right type of publicity and getting sucked into the wrong type

- Not knowing how to use the Internet to position yourself

- Not getting coaching and advice from someone who knows and understands the nuances of publishing

- Not knowing that you have to work your butt off to keep your book alive

Out with the Old, in with the New

Smart authors and publishers clean out old stuff. And old ideas. When it comes to writing, and publishing, the fabulous concept you had a few years ago may need to be rethought, revamped, or, *gulp*, tossed out.

Before you leap into publishing, ask: Is the idea you have current? Leading Edge? Has it been done before and have you come up with a whole new twist? Or is it ... yawn ... old hat?

For non-fiction, would doing a survey spark up some interest? Is there a major trend in the news that you can hook into and use as a weaver? How about conducting interviews with controversial or "in the news" personalities? Or, facilitate a focus group that might reveal new thoughts, trends or twists?

For fiction, just how clever or unique is your story line? Is it more like a "fill in the blank" that is common in the formula books that litter book store shelves or is it a true page-turner? Have you spent some time with a creative writing coach that can accelerate your learning and imagination curves?

Have you thought about ways to capture your reader's attention? And, do you know who your reader is? Anyone who thinks, "Everyone is my market," is clueless; it will eventually sabotage positioning efforts.

 Our clients have heard us say countless times, "The more you niche yourself, the bigger your market becomes."

Become a big fish in a small pond. The expert. The visionary. The unique voice. By dumping ideas that aren't working, scenes that don't click, you will become a new you, and an author that demands notice.

Publishing takes time. And money. It pays big time to get coaching and help yourself. Each of us has been there, and done that. Each of us has published traditionally, with a small press, and on our own. We are someones who have been there, done that. You don't have to do it, or go it, alone.

MONEY TALKS …
DO YOU LISTEN?

There's excitement in the air, the crowd is hushed, your belly is doing flip flops and the announcement comes. Holy smokes, you've won the Edgar, the Caldecott, the National Book Award … then you wake up. Dreamland is over.

Most authors we know and work with think big. Their little book could be "the one." Each year, book awards go to someone, and that someone could be you. It's truly amazing how many authors garner awards, yet have little else to announce their success. If your goal is to only get recognition and an award or too, then you might hit it. There are numerous local, regional and national book award contests that will welcome your book and entry fee.

We suggest that you refocus a tad. Yes, it would be wonderful to come away with accolades for your tome. But we think it's critical that you understood the business of publishing from the get-go; how to crunch the numbers to figure your breakevens; and be successful financially. The publishing grand slam homerun.

For starters, let's crunch a few of the numbers. Let's say that your book is a hardback and published with a mainstream publisher. If your book has a $25 retail price on it—your royalties are $2.50 per book for the first 5,000 copies sold and the next 1,500 will pay you $3.15 each. If you sold 6,500 copies, your payday would be $17,225, assuming your royalty was based on the full retail book cover price. If it's net, meaning the publisher calculates your royalty based on the net amount it receives, that amounts to less than $8,000. Depending on the discounted amount, it could be a little more, or less.

If you are doing a trade paper, royalties will be in the six to nine percent range. Again, you've got to pay close attention to whether it's based on retail price or net.

This doesn't take into consideration hold-backs, reserves, any special sales or the simple fact that most publishers only pay royalties twice a year based on the previous six months sales. It's common to hold back a percentage, the reserve, as a "just in case"—just in case books are returned from bookstores. In other words, the publisher may say that 6,500 copies have been sold, but there is a "but." Sold books and ordered books sometimes are put in the same language bin.

What happens if Barnes & Noble ordered 6,500 copies, "but" returned 6,000 of them a few months later? They didn't sell. If the publisher had paid the author on the "ordered" books, assuming that they will all sell, what do you think the odds are that an author would enthusiastically return the money to the publisher if they didn't? Be real, they aren't high. That's why 100 percent of earned royalties are not fully paid out. It's the reserve factor. And, returned books are quite common in bookstore chainland.

The New, New Way to Publish

The great majority of authors don't write a book within a few weeks or a couple of months. It's a rare author who is so highly organized and efficient that can pop them out that way. For most authors, the amount of money that is received/earned, if there are any sales, begins to look nominal when they consider the time and money spent on creating their masterpiece.

Alas, many authors who had published within the traditional publishing community are breaking ranks and going out on their own. With their established names, and brand, they've discovered that they can net more money, with less grief and more control by publishing themselves. How much more?

With the example above—if the author had been able to directly sell to their client/reader base, bypassing bookstores (remember, having a book listed on Amazon counts just fine—Amazon sales represent 20 percent plus of all book sales), that maximum of $17,225 could have yielded $162,500 minus production costs plus any coaching/shepherding of approximately $24,000, or $138,500. Which would you choose: $17,225 or $138,500; or something in between?

In the previous chapter, the top seven ways to publish were identified. Our goal is to do a rough breakdown so you have an idea of what your costs are and what you can expect to receive in sales revenues.

Below are approximations and averages to get to the bottom line. For example, each of us has worked with a variety of printers over the years. We normally advise an author/publisher to get at least three printing bids before they make a final decision. Sometimes it's not all about the cost per unit/book—the book may have special illustrations, tables and charts or a cover design that would be more suited for one printer over another, even though that printer was the high bidder. Based on our experience, we know a book that has just a few copies printed will cost more per unit than one that has had a few thousand printed. Sometimes, it's a dollar more; sometimes, several.

 Publishing is a business. Period. Whoever owns the business, wants to make a profit. If you publish through a traditional publisher, it wants your book to sell lots of copies—to make a profit. If it doesn't, your publishing career may become mud.

What if you wanted to open a Sally's Sewing Shoppe? Wouldn't it make sense that you knew about sewing? About the machine and how it works? Maybe an inkling about fabric types? How about sewing accessories?

Patterns? In other words, you need to learn about the business. Publishing is no different.

When you self-publish, and you contract with an AuthorHouse, iUniverse, Xlibris or a LuLu, you are sharing the profit. Their name is on the door, not yours. Whoosh—with the use of their name, you could see 50 percent plus of your profits exit overnight just because you used their name ... and you didn't think you knew enough to do it yourself ... or your didn't think you had enough money (or didn't want to) to front the startup expenses of your publishing enterprise.

With self and independent publishing, you are opening a business. If Sally's Sewing Shoppe needs a sewing machine repair person, a seamstress or a specialist in designing kid's costumes, it hires a person who can fill the bill on a fee basis—each job has a cost to it. Hopefully, the cost of the services will be far less than the revenues that are created. What's left over is the profit. Yours—all of it.

It's the same in publishing. Seamstresses, sewing machine repairs and kid's costume designers can be likened to editors, cover designers and printers. You have a job that needs to be done; they bid on it. You hire who you want and pay them on completion. You don't share your profits with them.

When you use today's modern vanity presses—LuLu, AuthorHouse, iUniverse, Xlibris, etc., your profitability is severely limited. As the owner of Sally's Sewing Shoppe, you could hire, and fire, vendors and suppliers. You make all the decisions. If you don't want to work with or use someone, you go somewhere else. It's still your place, Sally's Sewing Shoppe. When you publish through anything that doesn't have your name, you lose that option. You get to start over if you decide you don't like the establishment. New ISBN, new files, new cover design—new, new, new. More money, more money, more money.

When POD (print-on-demand) entered the publishing world, publishing blew wide open. Unfortunately, it has created a trap for many. The author ends up paying for 100 percent of all services—editing, cover and interior designs, illustrations, printing—you name it—and the vanity/

POD gets to split the profits with its name on the door, little money, if any at risk ... and they own the ISBN for your book.

What's the hook that gets the author?—usually the ability to do a few books at a time; the perceived reduction in the cost of fronting the publishing experience; and the ability to have a named wholesaler/distributor for their book. That's it. So why do thousands publish this way? Simply, they don't know any better.

Today's vanity press and POD publisher knows from the get go that the author that comes to them may have low financial expectations. He or she just wants to "publish" a book—making money and profits are not the primary motivator. Some are even so bold as to openly say that authors know that their chances of making money by publishing are as remote as winning the lottery.

We don't believe that in a minute—each of us has been quite successful within the publishing game through our books and with our clients. John has a Publishers Hall of Fame on his website and both Rick and Judith have consulted and coached many, many authors who have made significant moneys via publishing on their own.

If, and it's our opinion a very big "if," you are the rare bird who isn't into making money with your book, you still want it to look decent, and not something that was glued up at the kitchen table. That means that somewhere, in those pages, there's a desire to look good, be good, or do good!

Which Is You?

As a publisher, which general category do you land in?

Are you a hobbyist or casual author/publisher? Meaning that you will have minimal moneys to front various components of the publishing process—you are in the "do-it-yourself" side of publishing. As the cook and dish washer, you do much of the design work yourself and rope in others to do big expense items like editing via bartering or getting your friend who teaches English to do the honors. Your choice of printing will be digital and print-on-demand. You may opt to print one book at a time, in batches of less than 100 copies or go for a short run, usually less than 500 copies.

Online publishing may be your Siren. If it is, you have to invest in an infrastructure to support online sales—meaning websites, credit card processing and a marketing campaign. Cover and interior design costs are minimal and printing costs are not on your menu. The buyer downloads to his reader device or computer and if a hard copy is desired, the "print" command is clicked on.

Physical book publishing requires you to step up to the plate. Your product should be quality on the interior as well as the exterior. It's been professionally edited; you've put together a plan to create book sales and established a relationship with a distributor. Unless you are doing a short run for printing to "test" your market or seed reviews, your printing run will be 1,000 plus. The first real print break comes at 1,000 copies and numbers per unit start falling in larger print runs.

Number Crunching 101

Let's step away from the perceived prestige of a traditional publisher and compare apples to apples. You can only do this with the numbers—the amount of money that the typical or average author gets. The *New York Times* best-seller blockbusters—such as David Baldacci, Mitch Albom or Nora Roberts—are not the typical author. No, that person in the nonfiction vein will sell less than 6,500 books; for the fiction writer, it's in the 3,500 range. And that's in good times—in 2009, those numbers dropped dramatically.

The scenarios below represent a comparison of royalties that an author would receive via book sales from a traditional publisher and the author turned publisher, selling through wholesalers/distributors or within his own platform, meaning that 100 percent of book sales go to the author/publisher. Printing estimates are from offset printing. If digital printing was used, printing costs would be significantly less.

Assumptions:

The print quotes were obtained for a 256 page book that is 6 x 9 and 50 pound HiBulk Cream, offset (not digital or POD). Cover is laminated, freight from Michigan to Colorado, and includes content and cover proofs.

Our examples below do not include any costs for illustrations, cartoons, photos or any other type of artwork that would be used on the interior or cover of a book. If you do, you can take the frugal approach and use clip art or take it to the extreme and have custom artwork—always the author's choice. Nor do they reflect any consultants, coaches or book shepherds that were engaged during the process.

Percentages used for royalties paid to the author for traditional publishing are based on industry norms for a $15 trade paper and $25 hardback and based on net revenues (not full retail price), usually a 55 percent discount from retail price. Royalties range for the trade paper from 7 to 9 percent ($.47 to $.61 per book) and hardback, a graduated percentage beginning at 10 percent for up to 5,000 copies ($1.13 per book); 12 ½ percent from 5,001 to 10,000 ($1.41 per book); and 15 percent over 10,001 copies ($1.69 per book). Special sales are not included (which pay a smaller payout), nor are serial or foreign rights.

Warning! We advise all authors to pay close attention to any Royalty Clause—are royalties determined on net sales or retail sales? Retail will yield approximately double the amount of royalties received versus net. Many of the newer publishing contracts are based on net.

One other thing to keep in mind: the numbers below do not reflect marketing or PR costs if you engage in them.

Option #1 Traditional Publishing, Royalties Paid

We know, we know—many authors dream of being published with a New York House. It happens to thousands every year. Fantastic ... maybe. Option #1 shows why you should look before you leap. Traditional publishing's expectations of the author have changed significantly—when the author was courted, financially and emotionally supported along the way—it's a rare happening today. Celeb authors get the royal treatment—that's less than five percent. Most authors today are expected to create a great proposal in selling the book; write the book; and market/sell it like crazy. Sure, there may be a little publicity support, but don't expect much. It's up to you to move the book.

Most authors are looking at selling books in the 4,000 to 6,000 range. We've given you royalties for both trade paper and hardback starting with sales at 1,000 copies up to 100,000—at that rate, your publisher should be kissing your feet!

#1 Traditional Publishing – Royalties on Net	
Trade Paper at $15	Hardback at $25
7-9% Royalty paid to Author	to 5,000=10%; 5,001-10,000=12.5%; over 10,001=15%
$.47 - $.61	$1.13 - $1.41 - $1.69
Assumed 55% royalties paid on net discount	Assumed 55% discount, royalties paid on net

# of Books Sold	Trade at 7%	Trade at 9%	Hardback at 10 to 15%
5,000	$ 2,350	$ 3,050	$ 5,650
10,000	4,700	6,100	12,700
15,000	7,050	9,150	21,150
20,000	9,400	12,200	29,600
25,000	11,750	15,250	38,050
50,000	23,500	30,500	80,300
75,000	35,250	45,750	122,550
100,000	47,000	61,000	164,800

Option #2 Selling to Wholesalers - Distributors with 55% Discount

If your objective is to get your book into a bookstore or a library, you need some help. Wholesalers and distributors become your allies. Where wholesalers act as a go-between—bookstores can order books for their customers (or to stock)—distributors do the same and more. They pitch your book to bookstores, sometimes major media, libraries and other venues that sell books to the public. Distributors carry far more of your inventory than a wholesaler will. It's not a free service—both get discounts ranging from 50 to 60 percent off of the retail price (Amazon's Advantage program is at a 55 percent discount).

In either case, they expect you to be driving buyers to bookstores and to libraries so that requests are made for the book. This is what the Plan Thing is about … how are you going to get the word out that your book is hot; the answer to the problem at hand; or just a dawg gone good read?

#2 Selling to Wholesalers - Distributors with 55% Discount	
Trade Paper $15 with 55% Discount	Hardback $25 with 55% Discount
7-9% Royalty paid to Author	to 5,000=10%; 5,001-10,000=12.5%; over 10,001=15%
$6.75 net	$11.25 net

# of Books Sold	Trade Paper at $15				Hardback at $25			
	1,000	3,000	5,000	10,000	1,000	3,000	5,000	10,000
Gross	$ 6,750	20,250	33,750	67,500	$11,250	33,750	56,250	112,500
Cover	$ 1,000	1,000	1,000	1,000	$ 1,000	1,000	1,000	1,000
Layout -Editing	$ 5,000	5,000	5,000	5,000	$ 5,000	5,000	5,000	5,000
Printing	$ 3.17	1.66	1.38	1.16	$ 4.38	2.67	2.32	1.94
	$ 3,170	4,980	6,900	11,600	$ 4,380	8,010	11,600	19,400
Shipping	$ 271	631	833	1,510	$ 271	631	1,035	1,882
Total	$ 9,441	11,611	13,733	19,110	$10,651	14,641	18,635	27,282
Gross Profit	- 2,691	8,639	20,017	48,390	$ 599	19,109	37,615	85,218

Option #3 Independent Publishing & Selling Your Book on Your Own

You love bookstores, but you've got a thriving speaking business; do workshops and training for corporations; or you have a huge, and we mean huge, fan and friend base. You want your books to be available through bookstores, so you will probably seek a wholesaler relationship, but your goal is just to sell them. Through your website and what's called back-of-the-room sales. That means full price.

Before you look at the numbers, there are costs to think about. You may be lugging books around with you, or shipping ahead. You now have to think about fulfillment—processing credit cards, packaging and shipping. Of course, savvy person that you are, know to add an extra fee on top of the purchase to at least cover the handling costs ... yes?

#3 Independent Publishing & Selling Solo							
Trade Paper $15				Hardback $25			
# of Books Sold	1,000	3,000	5,000	10,000	1,000	3,000	5,000	10,000
Revenues	15,000	45,000	75,000	150,000	25,000	75,000	125,000	250,000
Costs	-9,441	11,611	13,733	19,110	10,651	14,641	18,635	27,282
Profit	$5,559	33,389	61,267	130,890	$14,349	60,359	106,365	222,718

Part of being an author, and publisher, is to understand the numbers. They speak ... and loudly at that. Comparing the three scenarios above, you get:

Summing Up ... Royalties vs. Wholesalers vs. Solo Selling								
	Trade Paper $15				Hardback $25			
# of Books Sold	1,000	3,000	5,000	10,000	1,000	3,000	5,000	10,000
#1 Traditional Royalties	$470 - 610	1,410 1,830	2,350 - 3,050	4,700 - 6,100	$1,130	3,390	5,650	12,700
#2 Wholesalers-Distributors	-$2,691	8,639	20,017	48,390	$ 599	19,109	37,615	85,218
#3 Publishing Independent	$ 5,559	33,389	61,267	130,890	$14,349	60,359	106,365	222,718

Numbers, and money, do talk. If you have a plan ... a platform ... that will move your books, option #3, Independent Publishing, is the way to go. It's work, no doubt, but so are all the other options. Don't kid yourself. And, with the extra cash flow, you could hire someone to support your efforts.

Know the Cost of Your Book

It's amazing how so few authors really know what their unit (book) cost is. Totaling the moneys that you spent for design—cover and interior—along with printing, shipping, editing, or any consultants you've worked with in the creation process, you come up with a sum. Take that amount, divide by the price of your book, and you come up with how many books you need to sell to "break even." Just know that number—how many books you need to sell—can take a great deal of pressure off your shoulders.

You may have 2,000 books in inventory. If your break-even comes in at 500 books, it's amazing the mental relief it is to many an author to know that they only have to move/sell 500 books to get their initial money back. The next book sale starts the profit train.

The Miscellaneous category could include the cost of your ISBN; packaging material for fulfillment or sending books for reviews; costs related to starting your publishing company; or website or social media related strategies.

Your Book ...

Title _____

# of Copies Printed _____

Cost of Cover _____

Cost of Editing _____

Cost of Layout _____

Cost of Art/Illustrations _____

Cost of Printing _____

Cost of Shipping _____

Cost of Consultants _____

Cost of Website _____

Cost of Marketing _____

Miscellaneous _____

Total Cost of Publishing: _____

To determine your cost per book, divide the *total cost of publishing* by the *number of books printed*. The result is your *cost per book*. In most cases, publishers will take just the cost paid for printing and divide it by the number of books printed—they figure that the cover, layout, editing, etc., is spread (or amortized) over the life and total number of books printed.

$$\text{Cost per book} = \frac{\text{Total Cost of Publishing}}{\text{\# of Books Printed}}$$

To determine breakeven number to recoup your publishing costs, divide your *total cost of publishing* by the *price of the book*. The result is the number of books you need to sell to recover your initial moneys. Our formula below assumes you get full price. If it's discounted and sold through retailers or wholesalers, the number needed to be sold will approximately double.

$$\text{Breakeven \# of Books to Sell} = \frac{\text{Cost of Publishing}}{\text{Price of Book}}$$

Our question for you: what can you do to reach your audience, crowd and fans to reach your breakeven number?

What's Next?

If you haven't already, then it's time to create a system to track all your expenses ... and profits. Don't forget keeping track of inventory. One system we like is Ron Watters' AnyBook—it's designed specifically for the small publisher. There's a no cost feature, coupled with a no time limit, to download the software and evaluate it. If, you like it after trying it out, all Watters asks you to do is register what you have and pay for it. Such a deal! Depending on what version you want, the AnyBook Publisher's Business Kit will range for $89 to $729. Information can be found at *www.RonWatters.com*.

If you are co-mingling your funds with your personal accounts, stop. You need a separate checking account. Get a Tax ID# from the IRS. Contact your state and get a resale license to peddle your books if you are at a local event. Start with the city that you currently live in; it may have a separate user license that carries an additional tax to it. You should be able to do all this online.

 When you learn to publish smart, treat it like a business vs. a hobby, with which you can achieve financial success. Crunching the numbers, negotiating with your various publishing service providers and knowing how many books you need to sell before you cross into profitability is all part of the picture.

YOUR PUBLISHING TEAM ...
SOLOING DOESN'T WORK

When we see authors turn publishers, we cheer. We, though, want to be enthusiastic cheerleaders. How's your book look? How does it read? Is it the best it can be ... or did you rush to publish, skipping a few of the steps, saving money, along the way?

Knowing what advisors and professionals you need along the way will save and make you money. Yes, you will have to spend some upfront, before you realize what the savings are and what your revenues can be.

We don't want your book to look, well, self-published. It's the kiss of death. It doesn't have to and creating it doesn't have to break your bank. That is unless you thought you were going to create and publish your masterpiece for $100.

> Think of the *Rule of 5* when creating your team of professionals and companies to work with: Your Cover Designer, Interior Designer, Graphics Designer, Editor, Illustrator, Website Developer, Printer, Book Coach or Shepherd, Agent or Publisher should be in the business of doing what they do for at least 5 years.
>
> There's a reason why people last—they are good. You don't want to start work with someone who is here today and gone tomorrow. Nor do you want to start with anyone green. As with anything, there's training and tricks of the trade that time reveals. Your preference would be for them to make mistakes on other people's books, not yours.
>
> The one exception could be in the artist, cartoonist or illustrator area. Talent is talent. Granted, it evolves. When you see artwork that appeals to you, it appeals. The only thing that needs a caution here is this: young artists, green artists, may not have the work ethic that you need to meet a deadline.

Let's look at key players in the publishing path:

Editors

Yes, yes and yes. All authors need editors—no matter how published and polished they are. In Chapter 6, *Publishing Requires Editing … No Exceptions!,* we go through the types of editors and how to engage one.

What's important here is to make sure you work with one that has edited, worked within your genre and one that you feel "gets" your work. If you don't feel that the editor is the right editor or that there are unseemly delays and hiccups in what you get back, get out. Some will advise that it's not wise to change editors in the middle of the publishing stream. We disagree. If the editor's pen doesn't fit, it doesn't fit.

The money issue will surface. If you feel that she has failed in delivering what she said she would and contracted with you for, or missed crucial deadlines, communicate so. You, we hope, can get moneys back. We suggest you state specifically, in any contract you make, deal breakers and consequences.

Rates for editors will vary. They can range from $25 an hour on up with $50 in the medium range. Some charge $75 an hour and you may think "theft," yet they could end up being the bargain—working several times faster than the one that charges less. Editors also can quote by the project.

The Graphic Designer (Cover Designer)

Experience counts when it comes to cover design. Covers are an art form—putting them together so that the art work, any illustrations, the use of fonts and colors, placement of photos or special design work requires skills that relate to books. Your cover is your primary marketing piece; your back cover should close the sale.

Designers will tweak and spotlight key words and phrases (with your assistance) so that they pop to the buyer's eye. Reversing colors, introducing new ones all add to the power of your cover. Getting the spine just right and placing barcodes, categories and prices all matter.

Don't shirk here. Even if the book will be printed in a POD format doesn't mean that you have to be in the mediocre ranks. POD doesn't create embossing or other enhancements that many covers have. It can, though, still look sharp. It's in the designer's hands.

Your costs will vary. Some designers charge a few hundred dollars; others thousands. Some by the hour; most by the project. Look at their portfolios. Do you love what they've done for others? Are there book covers you admire? Look in the Acknowledgment page and see if the cover designer is identified. Then start tracking via the Internet. If you have a dust jacket or a trade paper with flaps, the charge to create the cover is usually more—there's more "real estate" to design for. Makes sense.

Once you connect, brainstorming is in play. Most designers welcome your input—it's your book after all. You want to be proud of the exterior and interior. If the designer doesn't come up with a few ideas that begin to resonate with you, he may be the wrong fit. Make sure you have an escape clause if you need to move on.

When working with designers and artists, it's best to do it with contract and under a Work for Hire clause, meaning that payment will be made and that *the creative rights are now yours.* Don't trust that this can be transferred to you verbally, even if the designer or artist does so. Get it in writing.

Illustrators, Cartoonists and Artists

Is your book one that cartoons or an illustration of some sort would enhance? Do you already have originals or have you purchased cartoons that allow you to use them in a book format? Have you thought about how you want your chapter openings to look—just words that are the title or do you want an illustration of some sort.

Ken McAdams wrote *Bon Courage,* a story of how he and his new wife's honeymoon to a small town in France evolved into a full-blown love affair with the area. His wife, Bing, is a gifted artist. You can find her work on the cover and each opening chapter page. If Ken had had to "pay" for her art, he could have easily rung up several thousand dollars.

In Lynn Hellerstein's, *See It. Say It. Do It!,* extensive cartoons and illustrations are used to highlight activities that she's created throughout the book. In some cases, they are the difference between understanding what is written and scratching your head.

Bobbi Boldon created *The Princess Golf Handbook.* It's woven with humorous cartoons when coupled with the Princess' 50 Rules, create an amusing book. Funny without the cartoons, but a hoot with them.

Author Mara Purl specializes in women's fiction. Her characters live within and around Milford-Haven, a small fictional town on the Northern California coastline (*What the Heart Knows, Closer than You Think, Child's Secret and Cause and Conscience*). The covers are part of her brand—each distinct, yet connected and clearly Milford-Haven. What the artist delivers with each cover is postcard printable. Her fan club can easily recognize them, knowing if they've read the book or not based on the cover art.

If you engage an illustrator, make sure that communication is open with the interior design person and cover designer. They all need to be speaking the same language. Any artwork that is supplied for a book also needs to be run by the printer (your interior and cover design contacts will do this—don't complicate it by getting into the picture).

You can spend a mini fortune on illustrators and cartoonists. Here's where you want to negotiate like crazy. You can find gifted artists who are just starting out and desperately want to start their portfolios. You can outsource via groups like *www.elance.com* and put out a bid process and see who responds. Listing boards, such as Craigslist, might yield the perfect artist for you (that's where Bobbi Boldon found Don Sidle who ended up doing all the illustrations including the front and back cover art for *The Princess Golf Handbook*). A local art school may have budding artists interested in your project. Or, get the camera out and start pointing—you may capture the perfect photos.

If you plan on using the artwork in other forms or want it to be exclusively yours, be up front (versus allowing the artist to resell it). There may be an additional fee. Most artists charge by the piece and usage. If you have several that you want done, get your negotiating hat on.

Most of us are highly visual. Photos, illustrations, cartoons and nifty graphics can all add to the reading experience. If they are appropriate, use them.

Interior Designer

What's between the covers of your book is critical. Your layout says a lot about your book. We think of it as part of the eye candy. Here's what we look for:

- Is it visually appealing?

- For nonfiction, are there plenty of eye breaks with callouts, graphics, shading, photos, illustrations?—anything that invites the reader in and moves her through your words.

- Is the font and size of print readable or does the reader need a magnifying glass?

- Is there enough leading between lines (spacing) so that you don't feel that the lines are crammed?

- How about paragraph flow—are there widows or orphans? Meaning, are there one word lines or do pages end with one line that isn't a complete sentence or does the next page have a solo line on it and then start a new paragraph?

- Are any parts missing?—the Table of Contents says one thing but what follows doesn't match, is out of order or missing.

- How does each chapter open? Is it plain, or does it have drop lettering? Does it have any graphics such as an illustration or does it have a phrase or quote that might intrigue us? Is the chapter title font different from the main body of the book?

- Do the headers on each chapter match the Table of Contents? For that matter, are there headers?

- If there are bullet points, do they align?

- If there are photographs or other illustrations throughout, how do they look?

- If there are section or part breaks, how are they treated? Designers can come up with a catching layout that makes it standout, tying into your book theme or other illustrations.

Some authors are do-it-themselfers and try to cut corners. Just purchase one of the book software programs (Quark and InDesign are the main ones) and do it the hunt and peck way. We've seen authors go to print in a Word format. Don't do either. Your book warrants more—interior design, as with cover and editing, is not a do-it-yourself weekend project.

Working with the wrong, or inexperienced designer can be a book visual disaster. One client we worked with had completed her book; had it edited; the cover art fine-tuned and was ready to go to lay-out. She was referred to two professionals who had each done book interiors for over 20 years. Interviews were completed and she had selected her choice ... until her husband came up with a great idea.

His company created brochures for groups. He thought she should engage the designer they used. Unbeknownst to us, she decided to work with her husband's contact. She didn't know that there might be a difference between laying out a corporate brochure and a book; or that there were standard requirements on a book cover that a regular designer would know to include. And besides, it was a lot cheaper.

When we saw the book, we were shocked. Not only did we notice that there were widows and orphans throughout the pages; the dust jacket included hyphenating words from one flap to another; and that the book just didn't feel right. It included mixed up headers; variances in how chapters were opened; the deletion of key book requirements on the back cover; the copyright page had been altered and the margins were out of whack.

She was so excited about finally getting her book, until she too, noted that it didn't look or feel right. When she had told us that she would be using a different designer than the one that we had recommended, we were certainly open to hearing and working with new talent. After being assured that this person did know books and that her husband's company had used the designer's services for years, we trusted she knew what she was doing. Wrong.

Her great book became so-so because of the errors. And she lost the ability to include it in bookstores because of the lack of the ISBN and other exclusions that the designer was ignorant of. *The Rule of 5* was violated.

Interior design work can range from the low side of $1000 (and that's low) to several thousand, depending upon the complexity of the manuscript. That's compounded with the changes and tweaking that the author and in some cases, book shepherd, ask for once they see the book laid out. Interesting, once the book is laid out, we've always been amazed at the new editing changes we want to have as well.

Book Shepherds, Book Coaches and Book Consultants

All should bring a background in publishing—as authors, publishers or publishing professionals. Chapter 5, *To Book Shepherd, Or Not to Book*

Shepherd? … That Shouldn't Be Your Question offers an in-depth view of book shepherding and coaching.

Any book consultant should focus on the author's agenda. It's important that the author's voice and vision are honored and their budget respected. The result is a book they are proud of, not a book they regret.

Printers

Your book will be printed … either on paper or electronically. Many printers specialize is certain books; size of print runs; digital; offset; color specs; cover specs—you name it, it's out there.

Everything we've said above relates to print books except for editing. No matter which format you use, you need editing.

When talking with printers, it's wise to get several samples of books the printer has already produced, specifically books that will be similar to yours. Phil Knight has worked with Color House Graphics for years. His advice, "Do your homework in the pre-selection process but don't request quotes from more than 3-4 vendors. Ask the printer what resources and support they provide to small publishers or self-publishing authors. And, keep in mind, a low printing price does not always mean the lowest cost or best value." Knight's savvy words are all about doing your homework before making a commitment.

Remember the woman above who used the wrong designer? Ditto for printing as well. Her husband also had a great printer and one that was local and one that assured her that they could deliver the books to meet her schedule. Unfortunately, she didn't ask the company if they had printed real books before. She had seen the quality of the printing of the corporate brochures. Surely, this would be no different.

Wrong, wrong again. She figures this wrong turn cost her $15,000. And the company had to print it twice, printing it on the wrong paper— all glossy—when the book had activities that needed the reader to write it in (glossy is the wrong choice). Its press wasn't designed for a book format; paper slipped; pages were crooked here and there. Not a good day, or experience, for a newbie author.

You need the right printer for your book. The *Rule of 5* was again violated above. The company was indeed in the print business, just not book printing. Pass, pass, pass.

Tom Campbell of King Printing strongly believes that authors and publishers need to crunch the numbers and look realistically at sales projections. Too many times, the number of books printed is based solely on the price versus actual need.

According to Tom, "The industry for years has purchased their printing based on a margin model. The more printing you purchased, the lower the unit price per book. The problem with that model is that if the book did not sell or you had multiple titles that did not sell this was dead inventory. Traditionally this type of inventory would be scrapped or left unused in a space that cost money, adding even more cost to the original investment. A true measurement of the financials is—how many times does your inventory turn per year."

Digital printing is used for short runs—100, 200, 500—small runs. They aren't used for larger runs. There is a difference in the quality of the print. All you have to do is compare a digitally printed book with one done on an offset press and you will note that the digital is not as crisp as the offset. But, for fast reads (think airplane), it's perfect. Digital is used for mass market books.

Offset press printing is designed for larger runs. Many authors think that New York publishers print tens of thousands of books at a time—for every author published. Wrong. Huge print runs are created for blockbusters. Blockbusters aren't the norm. The norm in 2008 and 2009 was less than 5,000 books sold. That means that you, small publisher and author, are just as solid as a traditional customer with printers.

Whether you print digitally or offset, there are many fine printers to choose from. Some do both. We've had good feedback from many that we've worked with: Friesens in Canada, Four Colour in U.S. and China, Sheridan Books, Color House Graphics, Thomson-Shore, King Printing, Lightning Source, and Total Printing Systems are just a few.

Check the Resources in the back for a very partial list of printers and contact information.

eBooks usually don't incorporate graphics, callouts, illustrations, cartoons and photos. That was pre-iPad. iPad kicked off the next generation with its inclusion of graphics and color. eBooks that are sold as PDFs on author websites and not through the various platforms that Kindle, Nook, iPad, Smashwords and others generate, are usually done in a Word format. They can have illustrations and graphics since they don't have to deal with any conversion factors—they are PDFs.

The question that many have asked: will eBooks replace printed books? We strongly feel no—eBooks are an option. They will definitely be preferred by some; and rejected by others. We do expect them to expand their percentage of sales in the overall book market, but, as Tim Hewitt from Friesens summed it up, "There is no replacement for the beauty and tactile feel of the printed word."

When we asked him whether he saw eBooks causing a major blow to paper printers, he commented, "The largest printers will be far more impacted by e-books since the titles from the likes of King, Cornwell and Crichton are a far better fit for a digital read due to the disposable nature of their books."

If your book is one that has tools; quizzes; tables or graphs; is one that buyers highlight or markup with post-its; or one that a reader would pickup to reference often, print will be your choice. It most likely won't be the only choice, but it will be one that you want to produce.

When you ID a few printers that meet your criteria, get a few bids as Phil Knight of Color House Graphics recommended (and as we do). Then compare. If it's offset printing, you will have your books in four to six weeks. You will find that price breaks become apparent when you go over 1,000 copies. If it's digital, your books arrive in just a few. Overseas printing adds to delivery time because of transoceanic shipping via boat. The number of books you are printing will be a factor.

Websites and Website Designers

It's an online world and if you want your buyers to find you, you need a presence. This could be a chicken/egg thing ... which do you get first: the website or the designer? If the designer, he can start work before you obtain the URL (but you will have to get one). If you get the URL, park it until the designer is ready to start dropping his work into it. Preferably, the sooner the better.

 Don't expect the website designer to create content for your site. That's your job, or someone you hire.

Many websites have extensive questionnaires they use in the process. For authors, they can be hair-pulling—so many questions, so much detail. Designer Marty Dickson calls them Pre-Flight Questionnaires (*www. HereNextYear.com*). His clients have them completed before he sits down with a face-to-face or phone-to-phone planning session. Besides generic information, Dickinson wants to know color preferences; tag lines or mottos; ideas for you on have how you want your Home page to look; what websites you think look awful; what websites do you think are hot; do you have a video (Good idea—if there is a video on your site, the average visitor visits for six minutes vs. less than a minute without one.); do you have logos and graphics; will you sell your book off of the site? And, so much more.

The cost of developing a website is all over the map. If you want to do it yourself, you can. From little to no initial set up fee, you can investigate *www.Intuit.com* where, at this writing, it was offering a $4.95 a month version plus annual hosting fees. American Author has created a very author friendly template (in fact, it was designed for authors) for less than a $400 start up and $29.95 a month thereafter, which includes hosting (*www.AmericanAuthor.com*). Tech service is available and you've got a live person to hold your hand as you work yourself though the tutorials or have any hiccups in the process.

Private designing can range from $1000 on up. The price will vary on what you want and how much time it takes to create it.

Most authors want some control of their site. They don't want to wait until the "web guy" can queue them up to fix the problem if one occurs, or add/delete content to the site. On top of it, the cash register rings every time a request is made.

Today's websites are now being built on platforms that the owner can access and make changes in. Usually not in the design overhaul, but in the "addition to" category. The blogging platform, WordPress, is one of the most commonly used.

It takes many hours to compile content and it takes many hours to think through how you want your site to look and feel. Don't rush it, but put it on your must do list.

Distributors

If you publish your book and your intent is to make it available through bookstores and/or libraries, you need a distributor. Some distributors represent a variety of genres; some are selective. New Leaf Distributing Company (*www.NewLeaf-Dist.com*) is known for its representation of books within the body, mind, spirit and new age markets. Midpoint Trade (*www.MidpointTrade.com*) is more general— body, mind and spirit is just one of hundreds of categories of books it represents. The largest distributor is Ingram Publisher Services (*www.IngramPublisherServices.com*) which supplies to a variety of retail customers, wholesalers and libraries.

They want physical inventory which enables them to ship quickly to a store without waiting for you to ship to them and that they, in turn, must ship. Waste of time. Most distributors desire at least a six month's inventory (it's guesstimated) to work with. To Midpoint Trade, that means at least 500 books.

Working with a distributor means that you are going to sell to them at a discount. The industry standard is 50 to 60 percent discount. The publisher usually pays the shipping costs to and from the distributor's warehouse, although some distributors foot the bill for return inventory back to you (meaning it didn't sell). It will be in your contract. Distribution contracts will have termination and return-ability clauses—read them.

A Distributor has a marketing presence and its sales team will attempt to get your book into book stores, including chains. Some pitch to national media.

 If your goal is to have a Distributor represent you, or Wholesaler carry your book, you *must* have a decent marketing plan. That plan includes strategies for you *exposing* your book to *drive* people to bookstores to buy your book. If you don't, forget this path.

Wholesalers

Do the same discounting to "stock" your book, but don't do any pitching or marketing of it. Think of it as a more passive relationship. As with a Distributor, a Wholesaler wants to believe that you are going to hustle and drive buyers to bookstores, which in turn will order books through them. One of the largest is Baker & Taylor (*www.BTOL.com*). If stores and other outlets don't order books, expect them to be shipped back to you.

Fulfillment Centers

Orders are coming in—usually for one or two books at a time. Someone has got to process the moneys for them, package the book and ship it out. In most cases, the new author-publisher does the fulfillment piece. For some, it's no big deal. For others, a drag. You decide. There are fulfillment companies that will hold inventory and do the order fulfillment so you don't have to. Some process the money taking; some require you to do it.

If you enter into an arrangement, make sure you understand all the nuances and costs. Even if the fulfillment company is within your region and you want to pick up books, they may not let you. Instead, they ship them (meaning you incur costs—not a good idea).

Our advice is to read the small print and get references. This is one where we would definitely go to Google and put in the company's name with the words "complaints, problems and/or scam" after it.

Publishers

The publishing menu is vast. You have to ask yourself:

- Do you want to sell your book to a traditional publisher? If so, you may need an agent.

- Do you want to publish with a vanity type press?

- Do you want to publish in the eBook format?

- Do you want to pay a lump sum upfront, pay-to-publish, and have someone else do all the work to get your book to print?

- Do you want to work with a packager who coordinates everything from editing to design to printing?

- Do you want to publish it yourself, but don't want to put a lot of money (and/or time) in it, at least for now?

- Do you want to publish it yourself and are committed to selling books—lots of them—and being financially successful?

What is your preference? Each requires a different strategy, cost involved and time commitment from you.

If you are looking for a traditional publisher, preferably in New York, you will most likely need an agent. But, there are always exceptions. It's not uncommon for editors to scout writer's conferences looking for new authors. Many will offer face time for a few minutes—do it. Remember the 3Ps here: Pitch, Platform, Plan. When you can spiel that off within 10 minutes (which is a common meeting time allotted at a conference), you may just find your connection.

You can write a query letter. It's a start. Another option is to use the *Writer's Market*—the industry standard that identifies publishers in North America. It includes editor's names and their contact information along with genres published; what publishing imprints they have;

how many books are published each year; and what their submission guidelines are. It would be wise to verify that the contact information is still accurate and the editor still there before attempting to make contact. Do your homework.

Publishers routinely get truckloads of unsolicited manuscripts. To get around it, start with a query letter. If you are sending your query letter to multiple editors at the same time, state so. If an editor responds that he wants more info, you are no longer deemed unsolicited. Revisit what the Submission Guidelines are. Follow them.

Literary Agents

If you desire to work with a publisher other than yourself, one that is offering you a contract, it's usually wise to have a literary agent represent you.

Agents negotiate contracts—from advances; royalties; discounts that authors can buy books directly from the publisher; even moneys allocated to marketing. If you engage an agent, his job is to be your advocate, not the publishers.

References are important. If you know an author who has one, ask if you think her agent would be a fit for you. Referrals are always an advantage in getting your foot in the door. When published authors are happy with their books, their agents are routinely acknowledged within them. Some authors looking for agents have been known to contact agents via the backdoor—introducing themselves after they find the connection and pitching their work because of a like genre. Agents routinely speak at writer conferences. You might be able to get a few minutes of face time. You never know what works.

Writer's Digest magazine usually does a feature each year on agents who are accepting new clients and publishers who are looking.

Agents get paid when they sell your work. The contract that is negotiated will stipulate that all funds go through them first. They take their share, usually 15 percent, and forward the balance to the author.

Each year, agent Jeff Herman updates his excellent tome, *Jeff Herman's Guide to Book Publishers, Editors and Literary Agents*. It's a huge help for both the first time author and the experienced one who just wants to see who the players are and how to contact them. We highly recommend it.

Summing Up

When you develop a team that you can rely on, the publishing jungle is far easier to navigate through. It's easy to become overwhelmed. At times, you will feel you are slipping into quicksand. If you remember to work with publishing pros who are really pros—those that easily pass the *Rule of 5*—5 years in printing, editing, shepherding, agenting, publishing, covers, interiors, illustrating, distribution … anything that you might need to produce the best book you can, the number of snafus you run into will be dramatically reduced.

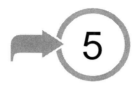

TO SHEPHERD, OR NOT TO SHEPHERD? … THAT SHOULDN'T BE YOUR QUESTION

When does it make sense to get a book coach, publishing consultant or book shepherd? Our answer is: unless you are experienced and a "pro" in publishing, get some help. Pronto.

Depending on where you are in the process, from being a flat out novice to someone who is breaking away from the traditional mode of publishing to anyone in between, a good book shepherd can make a huge difference in the turnout of not only your book … but in you.

Book Coaches, Book Consultants and Book Shepherds

There's a new breed of publishing consultants out there. Is there a difference between a book coach, publishing coach and a book shepherd? Most will say that they are the same. We think there are a few variables to distinguish one from another.

With each, being a guide to the author is critical. In the guide world, some plug ahead, leading the way; many interact, offering choices while giving you input to the pros and cons; and others encourage you to find your options and make a choice. Some are proactive; others reactive.

What you don't want is someone who is non-active. You can do that all by yourself!

Book Coaches are quite good at encouraging you (after all, who couldn't use a cheerleader or two during a challenging process?). One of the unwritten rules in most "coaching rule books" is that the coaching client is not given specific directions on how to do something or solve a problem. The coach doesn't have a specific agenda with a point 1, 2, 3. You get to determine the final solution. Many times, coaches respond to your statements/questions with questions.

> I need a cover designer for my book …
> *What resources do you need to find one?*
>
> I hear that it's important to begin a Blog for my book …
> *Good idea, what would you call it? How do you think you would go about creating one?*

Coaches keep their authors focused and work with them to develop strategies to get to whatever the next thing is sought. And that's a good thing. They do it with discovery and dialogue … moving the author through the process by listening and holding them accountable. They may do this with a variety of tools they use from the bag of tricks/experience.

If the author said she needed to connect with a cover designer within the next two weeks—the book coach expects that to happen and hold the author's feet to the fire when the two weeks are completed.

The book coach's goal is to get the author to his or her goal … whatever the goal is. They don't set the agenda for getting there, that's what the author does.

It's not unusual for successful authors knowledgeable in the intricacies of publishing to call themselves "Book Coaches" as they share their experiences in publishing with a novice author. While valuable information is shared, frequently the author is required to adopt the system developed by the expert book coach. A potential obstacle to their mutual success may be a lack of understanding on how individual authors receive, process and incorporate new information—something that takes time to develop.

Book Consultants are not so interested in working with you in the nitty gritty details of book authoring and publishing or guiding you in the development of your book. Nor are they so into dealing with whatever hiccups you are encountering that are creating roadblocks. What they do do, though, is tell you what to do, step-by-step to get where you tell them you want to get to.

> You need a printer—*here are three to contact.*
>
> You need a cover designer—*here are three that work well for your type of book.*
>
> You need an interior designer—*there's only one I like, call her...*

You get the picture.

Book consultants often create a program—a process that they have crafted telling you how to succeed. Many promote and present at seminars and workshops ranging from one to five days. Workshops that are designed to tell authors how to write, publish and sell books—but don't necessarily show them how and rarely give personalized attention assisting authors through the publishing and marketing process.

If you are a self-starter and don't need any monitoring or ongoing appointments with the consultant, you can save money using a book/publishing consultant. That is, as long as you are someone who can take on the "to-do" list and don't require much hand-holding or brainstorming during the process.

Book Shepherds have a depth of experience within the publishing and writing fields (as an author and/or working within the publishing field with authors); has connections with vendors and associates that will bring your book concept and vision to life; the ability to assist you in creating the actual book; someone who has marketing moxie and understands book selling—the alternative and niche markets; understands the business of publishing; and someone who is an enthusiastic coach for your "baby."

Not only will they "show-you" what book publishing and authoring is all about … they will "tell you."

Book Shepherds work with the authors to build a strong foundation—teaching them about publishing; creating a blueprint with timelines to meet goals; and then implementing a plan of action to meet deadlines and those goals. They should offer protection to the author … keeping him from making mistakes that could lead to thousands of dollars in losses, not to mention time down the drain. Book Shepherds want to create a book that looks good, feels good and that the author takes great pride in.

They know the experience of book birthing is similar to the labor of birthing a baby. Hard work; sometimes much pain. But in the end, the pain and agony have subsided to an unbelievable afterglow of delight. The book baby was worth it.

Book Shepherding is an author-centric approach focusing on the author's agenda; discovering the story behind the story; and revealing resources most author's don't realize they have. The goal is to ensure the author's voice and vision are honored; their budget respected. The result is a book they are proud of, not a book they regret.

What Book Shepherds Look For

As a Book Shepherd, Judith looks at a multitude of areas when evaluating an author and book project. All done to help decide whether she will take it on. These areas include:

1. *Does the idea or manuscript have legs?* Does it make sense, is it media worthy? What makes it unique so that it can shine within the same genre it's written for?

2. *Is there is niche for the book?* She hopes so—her philosophy is that the more you niche yourself, the bigger your market becomes. Much better to be the whale in the pond vs. the sardine in the ocean. When you develop a niche market, you become the go-to person—for media, for consulting, for speaking, for books.

3. *Has the author done any research to support the concept?* Writers should be doing research … even the best of story tellers have to

dig down, learning the craft as they weave their words of magic—background, arcing and storylines all have components that are rarely pulled from the air. Surveys and studies often become the basis of best-selling non-fiction. Some research is incredibly in depth; others more casual. Research brings in other voices—voices that the author can question, compliment or shred.

4. *Is the author, for non-fiction, an expert in the field?* This doesn't mean that he or she has to have academic degrees—it means that there has been an investment of their time in the topic area, and that the "degree" could very well be deeply engrained in experience. If you are writing a book about social media: Do you work in that field for a living? Are you recognized as a "go to" person by peers, the media or clients you work with? Have you already been publishing articles or speaking at conferences? Or are you someone who likes to spend a few hours every day on Facebook and you think that qualifies you as the go-to social media expert?

5. *Is the author prepared to invest her time, energy and money into developing and supporting her book?* Ahhh, the $64,000 question. Is the author a hobbyist or casual author ... or someone who intends to expand her business or build one around the book? Does she plan to be successful? To create a successful book, all three are needed. Your time—the project is not going to be completed overnight. Your energy—the creation, development and birthing of a book is equivalent to a full time job—do you have the commitment?

6. *Does the author understand what a ROI is ... a Return on Investment?* Will she be stymied by the overall costs of a book—from pre-production through post-production? Does she embrace books and publishing as a business ... or is it an encounter of the casual kind.

The POD market is huge and has fueled the expansive growth in self-publishing in recent years. But printing-on-demand is a oncey, twosy kind of affair. The cost per book unit is often so high that attempting to sell the book in a retail outlet results in a loss. Some POD's quality is so flimsy that bookstores won't carry the book. Ouch! Unless the author has a crowd to sell to, sales will be minimal. Understanding ROI is critical.

7. *Does the author really know what his book is about?* Hmmm, we know lots that are authored, but sometimes we really wonder if they were authored by the person whose name is on the cover. Or, we know the author is the author, but the book appears to be a mish-mash of ideas all thrown together without true development.

8. *Does the author have a platform or a following that will support the book—creating book sales and beginning the buzz building?* Just how do you plan on selling your book? On getting the crowd to come to you? Too many authors fail by simply believing that if they wrote it, printed it, they would come. Wrong. You've got to reach out, connect … you've got to do the work to connect with others and start the buzz machine.

9. *Has the author thought about, or written, a plan on how the book will be marketed?* This question should probably be #1—without having a plan on how you are going to create, launch and roll out your book, you are short a paddle or two in your book canoe. You may think you've got the plan all worked out, but with coaching and shepherding, that plan could very well take on a whole new life.

10. *If the author is a parent, spouse or partner, is there support for the project?* Without it, authoring is a lonely road to be on. There are times when you need such focusing and attention to the book, that little else gets done. Family and colleagues need to be in the loop. They are either for you or against you. The former is superior to the latter!

11. *Does the author need life coaching to support the creation of the book and being successful?* Authoring can be overwhelming. The process of creating the book, birthing the book and then marketing and selling the book can take its toll. Families are involved; work colleagues get involved and of course, the author. Reality checks are needed along the way.

12. *Does the author have a vision of what the book should look and feel like?* Does she have a vision of herself being successful with it? The creation of a book can be incredibility draining—it's easy to sometimes wonder why you are on this path (still). When there's a vision as to "why" you are doing this—you've got the answer to a major problem; your stories are a hoot and you've been told by zillions to get them out there; people are begging you to share your expertise so that they can access it easily, etc.—you can stay on target during the creation process so much more easily.

13. How best does the author *learn?* The Book Shepherd is the master teacher. To be the most effective, she needs to be tuned into learning styles—not only in communicating with her author; but in guiding the author in his own writing style. If she can't connect with him; the value of her expertise diminishes. If he doesn't write in a style that connects with his target audience; the value of his expertise slips away.

14. Will the author *listen?* And *follow-through?* There's a lot of work to this thing called authorship. The professionals that you will be working with have earned their stripes—they should welcome your input—but you should embrace theirs. When you work with a Book Shepherd, there must be a high level of trust that they will bring the right team together; guide you through the book publishing maze; and help you stay sane during the process.

Judith believes that one of her tasks is to train an author to be a successful author. She views each new author as part of the great book flock. It's just not bringing a team of publishing professionals to create the tangible book. It's much more. She combines life coaching techniques with her 30 plus years as an author and publisher to work with each author and book. And because of the intensity of the work that she does with an author in both development and publishing, she doesn't work with ones that exclusively work with POD. The commitment of the author isn't there; the philosophy that publishing is a business isn't there; and the ROI isn't there.

The best book shepherds we know have walked the walk, not just talked the talk. They are a combination of a maestro with a magnificent orchestra, and a creative director of an ad agency. Fine tuning; fading in and out soloists and groups during the process; adding the snap, crackle and pop soaring the score; creating smashing marketings; and at all times overseeing the entire process.

Nothing is free. Make sure you have a clear understanding on how they get paid, what time lines they work within and if they have expertise in your specific book area. Getting references is important. Not every coach, consultant or shepherd is a fit for your book.

Do your homework. Ask for a brief discussion about your book. Is there chemistry between the two of you? If the professional doesn't think your book rocks, it's the wrong fit ... there's got to be some enthusiasm.

Don't Get Duped

There are book shepherds, then there are book shepherds. There are many who call themselves book shepherds, yet they merely have some knowledge of publishing, or authoring, or marketing, or book publicity, or of blogging, or fill in the blank. Someone with a little knowledge and the right jargon can be downright dangerous.

A shepherd is defined as one *who protects, guides, and watches over.* That's exactly what book shepherds should bring to your book project. They won't write your book for you. But, should protect you from making senseless mistakes; guide you through the meticulous publishing process and watch over your journey from beginning to end. When it's over, you should feel that it's one of the best investments you've ever made.

How Book Shepherding Works

Book shepherds come in all kinds of sizes and shapes, providing a variety of services and charging a wide range of fees. At one end of the spectrum are shepherds that do similar work to that of book packagers. They literally take over the development of the book—rewrite or ghosting, editing, cover and interior design, printing, marketing and in some cases, PR. Your investment will range from $20,000 to $50,000 plus. That's a lot of money.

At the other end of the range, you can find a shepherd that is available as a coach on an hourly basis, for specific parts of your book project; at a per project basis; and some charge a monthly retainer. Depending on the time, your investment could be a few hours and a few hundred dollars to many hours and several thousand dollars. Caution: any book shepherd, consultant or publishing professional should disclose to you if they are getting kickbacks from people that they refer you to.

Be as clear as you can with what you need/desire. Get the arrangement in writing. What is this person really going to do for you? And, if it's not working, it's not working. Sometimes it's the chemistry; sometimes the "team" just doesn't click; sometimes what was promised isn't materializing; or you feel that it's not the right fit for you.

End it. It's over. There's no reason to continue your agony or mistrust. Make sure there's an escape clause in your agreement that is based on the shepherd's performance, including time frames for completion of your project.

Your book shepherd should bring passion, persistence, perception, planning and publishing power to the table. Judith has been shepherding authors for years. With over 25 books published, 19 with major publishers and the remainder with the imprint she created, she understands the authoring experience and the demands of being a publisher. Her detailed website on the process is at *www.TheBookShepherd.com*.

Her strategy is to "teach you" how to create your book and actively participate in the process. In some cases, when books have been abused or sabotaged by others (and sometimes by the author), she has stepped in to resuscitate and rescue it. She always feels a sense of wonder, as the author does, when the book is given a solid second life and look.

Among things that a book shepherd can assist you with are:

- Determining if there is a book, and who it is for;
- The tightening of your writing;
- The first run of editing;
- Shaping your book so that the finished product is visually attractive to the reader;
- Work with you to create cover copy that sings and uses marketing techniques to convert a book peruser to a book buyer;
- Creating the "hook" that makes you the expert;
- Crafting a proposal for potential sale to a publisher if that's your objective;
- The structuring of your PR game plan;
- Creating and shaping a speech that sells your book;
- Connecting you with the right printer;
- Connecting you with the correct interior/layout designer;
- Connecting you with or to the perfect cover designer;
- Connecting you to illustrators and cartoonists;
- Connecting you to foreign and movie rights agents;
- Connecting you to traditional agents;
- Developing eBook and other electronic strategies to expand your book's market;
- Putting the precise publishing team together for your book;
- Serving as the liaison between all team members;
- Getting you back on track;
- Developing your branding;
- Brainstorming your book launching;
- Connecting you with a distributor;
- Assisting you in developing strategies to balance the author life with your everyday life; and
- Much, much more … including all around hand holding.

With their huge circle of quality contacts, book shepherds will be the captains of your team, but insist that you come in as a "co-captain."

How It Works ...

You need to ask. Is it all by phone? Should you schedule time to be in the Book Shepherd's office? What about coming to your office? The answer will be: it depends. If you are someone that lives out of the immediate region, it will most likely be a remote relationship: phone, texting, computers and Skype. You and the Book Shepherd will decide what protocol is taken, including who calls who. Judith has worked with several clients that she never meets with in person because of location factors ... yet all the work gets done. Some distance clients will drive or fly in for the first session, then continue remotely.

Expect the first session to run two to three hours, depending on the complexity of what you need. For some, it's all they do need. They take the recommendations and run with it. Most, though, have additional follow-ups, usually lasting several months until the book is published and marketing, media and other post-strategies are in place. Judith and her partner, Katherine Carol, have created a unique tool called the SOURCE™ analysis that is implemented after the first meeting. From it, amazing insights are derived that help them, and the author, maximize each step in the process.

Successful books don't just happen by themselves. They need a plan ... a platform. Author Rhonda Spellman had neither... she thought she did, but after Judith spent two hours with her, it was clear that she was going nowhere fast. Over-extended, tired, frustrated and with too much money already misspent, it was evident that learning how to prioritize; creating a more compelling and succinct vision; discarding poorly designed material; and focusing was urgently needed.

Rhonda was put on a time diet—if she was going to be a client, she had to commit to abandoning time wasters—including hours on the phone and Facebook. She began to focus immediately on targeting her markets. Soon she had a top notch presentation, was listed on a national speaker's list and found her life began to balance as she morphed into a new life style, that of a successful author. In her words,

> If only I had brought you in at the beginning of the process …
> I would have saved thousands of dollars.

Her book, *The Journey: Home from Autism*, had to be rescued from herself—six months later, it birthed, started gathering recognition and awards and has positioned her as an expert in the field.

Best-selling NY Times authors like Connie Glaser, author of *GenderTalk Works* and *Women Who Swim with the Dolphins*, decided to take her own books back, revamp and revise them and republish under her own imprint. A fast study, she only needed a few hours,

> The two hours I spent with you were the single best investment
> I made in this whole process.

Being successful in publishing requires creating a strategy, something a Book Shepherd should excel in. Barbara Joye had self-published via print-on-demand (POD) a book that she was promoting, and selling, on her website. Its lack of sales, contrary to what she had envisioned, was beginning to erode her confidence and landed her in Judith's offices.

The big picture was developed around her vision of what she wanted and saw possible. As a result, she revamped the first book, *The Light Won*, making it far more attractive, readable and professional looking vs. the "drop it in a template and print it when needed" approach.

An additional manuscript for a second book (and third) was created from that first session. It expanded her initial big picture to include cover design, the perfect layout and printing format. *The Creating Formula* and *The Journal of Trusting* poured out of her. Barbara's bonus was her redefined vision that gave her a seamless, highly professional, readable books and brand. The additional books enhanced her credibility and expertise—and all with her branding look that launched her as a "player" in her genre.

Don't try to do it all yourself or alone. If you do, the end product—that book that you wanted and believed in—will look like it was a do-it-yourself project.

Summing Up

The Book Publishing Consultants and Coaches may focus on the aspect of just publishing—creating a book and getting it out there ... whether by a traditional publisher or by the author. They will most likely identify a variety of methods to use. Book Coaches often cross lines with a Writing Coach—guiding the author through the manuscript phase to the finished product. Both will usually recommend other publishing professionals to support the author's needs.

We like to think that the true Book Shepherd combines the two—creating a quality manuscript that leads to the book that in turn, leads to publication. And during the process, working with the author to create the over-all game plan—pre, during and post publication—for the book and the author.

When an author has a plan, the cost of using any consultant is reduced. The savvy author views publishing as a business, not a whim. She's committed. It takes money ... with the huge number of books being published every year, the Momism, "If you can't do it right, don't do it" holds up. "Schlocky" looking books can't compete with spiffy covers and interiors that flow and are eye appealing. It's just too hard to get past the cover in most cases.

We don't encourage authors to attempt to publish on a shoestring. If you are going to compete in the multi-billion dollar publishing business, the quality of what you present shouts volumes. Covers, interiors, editing augment the power of your words. Each speaking loudly.

Publishing is riddled with obstacles. Sometimes they are nightmares for the author. You don't need problems ... you want solutions. The Book Shepherd should supply them.

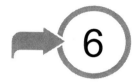

PUBLISHING
REQUIRES EDITING ...
NO EXCEPTIONS!

The difference between most self-published books and small, independent and traditional published books can be summed up in one word: editing ... or the lack of it. If your book is loaded with errors, the odds are that you've lost the reader. And your own credibility.

Every author needs an editor. Every publisher should only publish what has been edited.

Editing moves to the top of your list as your manuscript is completed. It requires a critical eye—yours and the person you hire to be your editor. Make sure the editor is the right editor—with the skills and experience that are needed to enhance your book. This doesn't mean that you don't create as clean a copy as possible before you hand it to your editor—do it.

We encourage you to have three books as companions during your writing process: *The Elements of Style* by William Strunk and E.B. White,

On Writing Well by William Zinsser and *Grammar Girl's Quick and Dirty Tips for Better Writing (Quick & Dirty Tips)* by Mignon Fogarty.

 Savvy authors and publishers create their own personal libraries for resources—don't borrow or get them from the library. You should own (and use) *The Elements of Style, On Writing Well* and *Grammar Girl's Quick and Dirty Tips for Better Writing (Quick & Dirty Tips)*.

For both fiction and nonfiction, there are a variety of "how-tos" out there. We are firm believers in studying the pros—what authors are consistently on the best-seller lists—who wins the big awards? Notice their set-ups, table of contents, flow. Most metro communities have a variety of writing groups, critiques and associations. Get involved.

Fiction writers would be well served to subscribe to Victoria Mixon's magazine, *The Art and Craft of Fiction.*

And, if you are thinking of stretching and creating a screenplay, Robert McKee's *Story: Substance, Structure, Style and the Principles of Screenwriting* belong on your bookshelf. The ideas within will take fiction writing to a higher level as well.

The What's-What of Editing

Copy and Grammar Editing

Copy editors out the typos, use correct punctuation and polish grammar. They make sure your pronouns match as well as the subject and the verb. Copy editors follow the grammar rules. As the author, pay attention to the use of active verbs (yes) vs. passive (no). Wise move: make sure that it passes your 6th grade English teacher's test—you want an A. This isn't a gray edit—it's black and white.

Line Editing

Line Editing is all about your sentences. Do they flow; is there structure and clarity; does it make sense and is it readable? The author's voice is evident—line editing reveals the years of experience that the editor brings to the table—sci-fi editors are most likely the wrong fit for the romance novelist—her tone, style and language techniques won't be in synch with the genre.

Developmental and Content Editing

It's a rare manuscript that doesn't need a little help. Some need to be trimmed; others expanded. Some need minor rewriting; others, major. Some need rearranging; while others, new gutting and new material added. For fiction, it could be for character or plot development.

Granted, some need a lot, but the question is: who do you call in? Editing ghost busters can make a book shine ... their editing skills are not so much black and white, more like: what's better and best. Phrases take on new meaning; sequencing and scenes make sense and flow; dialogue makes sense; and this is the phase where your manuscript doesn't grow in size, it usually shrinks. Redundancy is eliminated, sections may be repositioned and reduced; others expanded or greater detail given.

Proofreading

Proofreading is sometimes done by the copyeditor, sometimes a content editor and sometimes by someone who hasn't seen the manuscript. Your book is coming down the stretch, ready for layout and the printer. Because you and the editor have been so involved with the manuscript, it's unlikely you are going to catch remaining typos and punctuation. You just don't see it. Fresh eyes help.

 Hint: No edit is perfect. Reading your finished manuscript backwards and out loud reveals an unbelievable amount of "left-over" editing mistakes that easily slide under the mat.

Your editor should be on the alert for clichés and the overuse of words and phrases. Attention should be paid to words used to start a sentence (you don't want to use the same word as the first word in multiple sentences within a paragraph. And, for that matter—watch how each paragraph starts. Remember, the reader not only looks at the words, she looks at how your masterpiece is presented to her.

If you, as the author/publisher, haven't done so, this is where "eye candy" should come into play. Think of the reader—long sentences and paragraphs aren't appealing to the eye. Break them up.

In non-fiction, pages and pages of words without breaks make reading tedious. Use subheads, callouts, boxes—vertical and horizontal, shading, illustrations, cartoons, graphics to introduce sections and/or chapters. In other words, make it interesting. Fiction is a different animal. Readers expect chapters to flow on top of each other as long as the story—be it for kids or adults—grab them. Breaks, cartoons, etc., are important.

Saving Money

As the author, do as much of the editing as you can yourself. That will cut down on the time your editor will spend. For example, reading your manuscript out loud to spot the areas where you stumble and to find the string of paragraphs that all start with "I" or "So" or any word that is repetitive and could easily be substituted with another. Also ask friends to help read the manuscript at this stage, and don't forget to use a style manual for any area where you have a question.

The Rule of 4

Yes, you read the subtitle correctly. Reread your copy four times.

Your credibility as an author surfaces in the editing process. It's tedious. The same copy needs to be reviewed several times. To minimize mistakes sticking, avoid proofing your own copy. It doesn't work. New eyes are needed. It's amazing how reading backwards makes typos pop out—and reading aloud highlights garbled phrases.

The Rule of 4

1. Look for deviations—double words (than than), typos and odd-ball word breaks many software programs routinely hyphenate.

2. If you use math examples or columns of numbers, check and recheck your numbers. Look for poor phrasing pronoun agreements, subject and verb usage and repetition of words and phrases (use the Thesaurus). This is the *ruthless editing* part on your own verbiage.

3. Grammar, punctuation, capitalization and spelling come next. Pay attention to misplaced caps, which can easily sneak in after a proper capitalization (i.e. LIke).

4. Final read through is all about visuals. How does your spacing, indents, headings, subtitles or callouts look? If you used endnotes or footnotes, do the numbers match the text? Is the flow of the text easy on the eyes?

There is no getting around it—whether you are self-publishing or seeking a commercial publisher, your book will need some professional editing. But it's up to you how expensive the editing invoice will be.

Here are some tips to help you keep costs down as you work with your editor:

1. **Find an editor who understands the genre of your book and who has credentials or skills with books in your field.** Hiring a fiction editor to edit your memoir book, or a nonfiction editor for your novel will most likely result in more time spent editing ... meaning you pay more money.

2. **Determine what kind of editing you need.** Do you want the editor to provide copyediting (light), content or substantive editing (comprehensive) or something in-between?

3. **Ask your editor candidates to do a sample chapter that you've completed.** Pay attention to what is done—corrections, changes, or altering the tone of your "voice."

4. **Turnover as clean a copy as possible.** Spell check isn't perfect, but it's a start. Friends and colleagues can be readers. Ask them to be brutal as they read. Read it out loud—if you fumble over words, phrases or sentences, fix them. The cleaner the copy, the less money you will spend.

5. **Determine how charges will be assessed.** Until the editor gets into the project, it's difficult to know how long the editing will take. Guesstimates can be done. Most editors charge by project, by the hour, page or word. You don't want to be blindsided. Negotiate.

6. **Get references and copies of completed books that have already been edited.** Always. Check out the Acknowledgement page if there is one. Happy authors usually ID their editor with a kudo.

7. **Editing is a business, just as publishing your book is.** Your editor becomes part of your professional team—a friendship may evolve, but always keep in mind, you are hiring the editor to do a job, not paying her for friendship. If you are planning on being away from home or office during editing, let her know. And give an alternative number that you can be reached at if necessary.

8. **Tell the editor what you expect.** Be specific—ID what your goals are; and let the editor know if there are key words or phrases that are sacred and can't be tampered with or are unique to your book, including odd-ball spellings. If you are using endnotes or footnotes, point them out. Are there special callouts, use of lyrics (get permissions) or placements of photos, graphs, tables, quotes or phrases? You should be clear on who your audience is (you don't want your writing style to be for adults when it's supposed to be for juveniles), your editor should be able to "fix" the tone to match your reader.

9. **Delivery of manuscript—ask preference.** Most editors prefer to get a completed manuscript, including front (table of contents, acknowledgements, forward, preface, dedication, copyright page) and back matter (about the author, afterword, teaser for next book, appendixes, bibliography, end notes, glossary, index). Some will let you send a few chapters at a time. You need to ask.

10. **Does your editor prefer online or hard-copy editing?** Some editors want to work on hard copy; others prefer the digital version. Some want both. Determine who makes the corrections to the final copy. Just ask.

11. **When your editor speaks or marks, pay attention.** The great majority of the time, your editor will be right on with his recommendations. With few exceptions, follow them and make the changes. We recommend that when you get your edited manuscript back, definitely let it rest a day or two before you tackle it. Sometimes the edited changes seem so major, that they are overwhelming. Once you get into it, they will make sense.

12. **Discuss any deadlines.** Let your editor know if you are under a deadline for delivery to layout or a publisher.

13. **Communication is critical.** Don't just dump your manuscript and disappear. Check in with the editor to see if he has any questions.

14. **Think twice before getting a divorce.** If you are unhappy and you don't like what the editor is doing, terminate the relationship—the sooner the better. If you don't think the editor "gets" your book, bail. But, if it's an issue of poor communication, call a powwow and try to work it out.

15. **Written contracts.** If you want one, ask for one. Many don't work with written contracts or agreements, but rather within the stated proposal to you regarding fees. If you have one, include: timeframes, fees, what the editor's responsibilities are and what yours are.

 If you create words or use quirky phrases, we like the creativity. Give your editor a heads up so that she doesn't decide you are a blooming idiot when it comes to language. Who knows, it just may be the charm of your book that gets the buzz going.

Finding an Editor

You may know editors already. What they will not be is your best friend, your mother or your colleague at work. Unless; unless they do editing professionally. Most editors have a preference for what manuscript they prefer to work with. Fiction and cookbook editors are a different breed from self-help and children's.

If there is a website, check it out. Information on what they do and how they work will most likely be posted. It may reveal what hourly rates or project fees are. Interview them. Ask for names of similar books that they've worked on. Open up your favorite books. Go to the Acknowledgment page—it's a rare author that doesn't say "thank you" to their editor—Google him or her. Reach out to other authors you know—who have they used that they would use again (and not use again).

Most editors not only welcome a phone call or email; an interview to see if they are a fit for your book; but they normally will do a sample chapter or two so that you can see "their stuff" with your words. Pay attention to how they handle your voice (Did they make it their voice, converting from yours?). Yes, most editors are decent writers—one of their jobs is to make you look good on paper, a better writer. It is not to take over your book unless you hired them as a ghost—to write the book in the first place.

When you are shopping editors, don't be afraid to ask several of them to do a sample of a chapter or two. Few will charge. Do a comparison, than go with the one that makes your work sing and feels right for you.

If you are going to include an Index, it cannot be finalized until after your book is formally laid out—you aren't going to know the correct page numbers. And, once the book goes to the printer, hands off. Outside of a blatant typo, misinformation or monumental breaking news, resist the temptation to add a few lines here and there. When it gets to the printer, it's a print. The charges for changes at this point can be immense.

Summing Up

Smart authors use an editor who specializes in their genre, one that they trust. Editing is a process that starts with content editing followed by copy editing and finally proofreading—but only when the manuscript is "done." Don't push the process; proofing before content and copying can kiss off moneys. Editors don't know what you want—you have to tell them.

FRONT MATTER, BACK MATTER AND OTHER MATTER

The interior design of a book not only consists of the design of each page but the "flow" of the book.

Front Matter is similar to all the announcements before a meeting gets started: title; rules (copyright); any disclaimers; order in which the book will be presented (table of contents); special announcements (dedication, books previously written by the author and overflow endorsements); acknowledgments (although these sometimes land in the back of the book) and introduction.

Back Matter could include an appendix; tables; index; glossary; bibliography; footnote or endnotes (sometimes placed at the end of each chapter they appear in); about the author page (sometimes you may find this in the front matter); and information on other books, workshops or products that the author has. It could include a list of resources; references and bibliography; or a sneak preview chapter from the author's next book. It's anything that follows the last chapter of the book.

Other Matter includes the ISBN, Library of Congress number, barcodes, getting copyrights, pricing the book, bar codes category(s) that the book is in, decisions about how the cover will look and will the book be hardback or trade paper.

Front Matter

Front matter is easily identified as everything in front of your opening chapter. Number is different, usually in Roman Numerals. Common front matter would include in the order of appearance:

> Extra or Overflow Endorsements
>
> Half-Title page
>
> Title page
>
> Copyright page
>
> Books Also By … the Author
>
> Dedication page
>
> Table of Contents
>
> Foreword
>
> Introduction or Preface
>
> Acknowledgments

Back Matter (or End Matter)

Order is not as defined as the front matter. Usually, the footnotes and endnotes precede the index. About the author, any information about his workshops or product sales will follow. Your Back Matter will continue in the regular page numbering sequence.

> Footnotes/Endnotes
>
> Appendix
>
> Glossary
>
> Index
>
> About the Author
>
> Other info by author
>
> Other info by publisher
>
> Sneak preview of upcoming book

Other Matter

Your book will become a form of art. Your words, of course. But so is the presentation of it—the cover: back, front, spine, and if you have a dust jacket or flaps on the trade paper, those as well. What price you select, the categories you print on the cover, the hooks and grabbers for copy and whether you choose to include endorsements.

Pricing Your Book

If a chain store like Barnes & Noble had its way, every book would be priced under $15. Is that what your book is worth ... to your market? Maybe, maybe not. You want to price your book for what is inside it.

Have you created an amazing solution that millions want? Is your book designed for a niche market? Is it a professional book, one that the buyer might pay a higher price for? Is it a children's book? Hard cover or trade paper? Is it a big book—meaning lots of pages—or a mini book? Does it have color or is it black ink throughout?

Your book's true value is between the covers. Does it solve a problem; deliver a solution? Is it for business or for healthcare? Is it entertaining or belly laughing humor? Is it a unique gift book or designed for young children? Is it a suspense novel or chick lit? What is it?

We recommend you take a trip to your favorite book store. Go to the section that is your genre. What's the price range? How does what's on the shelves compare with what you are creating? Let your fingers do the walking through Amazon.com or BN.com. What's the price range, again in your field, of what's selling?

If bookstores will not be your primary selling platform, then what do you think someone would pay for yours? Better yet, if you were to hear about a book that is a clone of what you are doing and were open to buying a copy, how much would you be willing to pay?

Pricing can be a true fickle factor. Rick has primarily published with other publishers—they've set the price. His books are usually trade paper with a high selling point of $19.95 and low of $12.95. Amazon, of course, does discount. His books are mostly sold through bookstores and when he speaks, then they are sold at conferences. John's books range from $27.95 to 13.95 online, with discounts via Amazon and full price at conferences. He sells a significant number from his website. Judith's books are priced between $35 and $25. She's never been a proponent of the 95 or 99 cents club. Again, Amazon does some discounting. Most of her sales come from the conference arena with few from traditional bookstores.

Each of us have tested our prices to determine what our respective markets will allow. You need to do this as well. Then, you will know the price for your book. You can't control what Amazon decides to discount you to, if they do. If you post your book on Amazon, you will go with their flow.

There is a bottom line; one that too many authors turned publishers forgot to factor in. Let's go back to number crunching. In Chapter 3, *Money Talks … Do You Listen?* the various costs of publishing were identified. What is the amount that is allocated to printing? We look at a retail price that is seven to nine times the printing cost per book. If it's $3.10 per book, the retail price will range from $22 to $27. Can your book, your market, support it?

This is where so many authors in the self-published arena hit the wall. Because their print run is so small, the unit cost is higher. A $4 (and sometimes higher) cost per book cannot be converted to a $28 to $36 dollar price tag.

Getting Your ISBN (International Serial Book Number)

In the old days, ISBNs were free … that was in the early 2000s. RR Bowker discovered that there was gold in the publishing hills and started to charge. Today's ISBN is a 13-digit number starting with 978. You will place it on the back cover of your book along with a bar code that represents the number and the price of the book. You will also include the ISBN on your copyright page.

You can buy a single one from them for $125; a block of 10 for $250; 100 for $575; and into the thousands for more. We recommend you get a block of 10—if you revise your book, or create another, you need a new ISBN. There's plenty of information on the Bowker site, *www.Bowker.com*, where you can immediately purchase yours.

The sooner you get your ISBN, the better. You will need it when you apply for the Library of Congress Catalog Number (LCCN). ISBN's are your ID card to the book selling world. You must have one. And, when you assign an ISBN to a title, report it back to Bowker for inclusion in *Books in Print*.

Registering Your Book in Books in Print

Every book distributor and major book seller has a copy of *Books in Print*. With a few clicks, you, and your book title can be found. Orders can be placed from anywhere in the world. Once you have your ISBN, go back to the Bowker site and complete the registration for *Books in Print (www.Bowker.com)*. It's free.

Obtaining Your Library of Congress Catalogue Number

The Library of Congress Catalogue Number (LCCN) is also known as the Pre-assigned Control Number (PCN). If you want your books available to libraries, you need this number. Once you have your ISBN (you must have it to apply), you apply at *www.LOC.gov*—all free. You will also include this number on your copyright page.

The LCCN is constant. If you do additional editions to your original work, the LCCN remains the same; the ISBN will be new. The numbers are assigned to books that the Library of Congress assumes will be included in library collections.

Filing Your Book with the Copyright Office

Most publishers wait for their printed book to file it with the Copyright Office. Remember, your book is copyright protected even if you haven't filed it under Common Law. It becomes registered, when the Copyright Office *receives* it.

When you have your book, send a copy along with the TX form to the Copyright Office with $30. The TX form can be obtained at *www.loc.gov/*

copyright/forms. After the Copyright Office receives your book, money and form, its system takes over. Several months later, you will receive a photocopy of the official registration, seal and all. Some authors frame it.

Getting a Bar Code

You will need a bar code if you are going to sell your book in stores. Types of bar codes vary. The one used in bookstores is called the EAN 13 bar code. You can purchase one at the time you order your ISBNs or you can get one afterward through Bowker, or *www.BowkerBarcode.com*. We recommend that you have your book cover designer obtain and supply the bar code for the back cover of your book.

Identifying Your BISAC Subject Headings

When's the last time you were in a bookstore or a library and asked help of a clerk for finding a book? Most likely, she went to the computer, put in the title or a few key words, and sent you (or escorted) you to a specific section of the store or library.

The guide most likely used came from the BISAC subject heading the publisher selected and stands for Book Industry Standards and Communications. The Book Industry Study Group (*www.BISG.org*) updates its category list annually. Known as the BISAC Subject Codes List, it's a standard used by many publishers throughout the supply chain to categorize books based on topical content.

The list contains categories such as: Travel, Crafts, Family & Relationships, Business & Finance, Juvenile Fiction, Cooking, Nature, Body, Mind & Spirit or Humor and Reference. Categories have sub-categories as well.

The words you select will be the key words that are placed on the back of the book so the buyer can easily view it (often in one of the upper or lower areas of the back cover in a stand-alone format). You will also place it on your copyright page. We say—there's nothing wrong, in fact it's the norm, to select anywhere from one to three words to get your book to the right spot. If your vision for your book is to be in a library or a bookstore, it's a must have. The Subject Heading applied to a book determines where the work is shelved or the genre(s) under which it can be searched for in an internal database.

Lyric, Photo, Cartoon Rights and Citing Others

If you are using lyrics from a song that you didn't write, stop. Get permission. Don't even muck around with Fair Usage. Contact a rights representative and go through the hoops necessary—or at least find out the cost. Then, you can decide how important those four lines are to include in your work.

The use of cartoons can get you into trouble unless you have the right to use them and the cartoonist has granted permission. Ditto for photos and everything else you reproduce that you didn't personally create.

In citing another's written work, Fair Usage is a doctrine that permits use of copyrighted materials that are listed in the Copyright Act. Those include criticism, comment, news reporting, teaching and research. If there is any doubt, seek legal counsel and or the author's written permission. This is an area that it's better to be safe than sorry.

Just because it's on the Internet doesn't make it free. When in doubt, ask.

Hardback vs. Trade Paper ... Which?

If you love books, you probably keep them and prefer your favorites to be in a hardback format. Quick reads or something you most likely will not read again will influence you to get a trade paper version. How about your reader?

We love hardbacks too, but be practical. They are more expensive for you to produce and for the buyer to buy. Is there a strong market for it?

New authors and publishers always have questions as to what is needed and required and where the placement will be in a book. There are hard and fast rules and there is flexibility.

As you come down the stretch with your manuscript, take some time and explore a few books and note the format and sequencing of material as it is presented. An experienced interior design professional will also be a welcome guide.

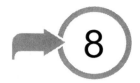

BOOK COVERS TALK ...
DOES YOURS POP ...
OR SNOOZE?

At a recent publishing conference, we talked with a gaggle of newly published authors. As proud as a new Dad or Mom, they put their treasure in our hands. Some, we ooohed and ahhhed over; many, we didn't. Too many times, the cover was poorly designed, didn't relate to the book topic and was third-rate at best.

Why, oh why, do self-published authors insist on creating mediocre book covers?

Covers Are Your Barker ...

Look at me!

I have the answer to your question!

Here's the solution to your problem!

Wahoo ... pick me, pick me ... I'm a terrific read!

Your book cover should have the same grabber as the "wow" billboard on the roadside. Can you think of some that grabbed your attention so quickly that it became an "aha" or made you smile? Did you get what the product was it was pitching? A cover that works IDs the genre and the subject of the book. It does it with words and graphics.

Covers are a critical investment in the presentation of your book ... not just the front, but the back. If you have a dust jacket or flaps, you've got more "real estate" to pitch to the book buyer. Where the front is designed to say what the book is about and convey, "Pick me up now, I'm the one;" it's the back cover that should get them to fall in.

Cover Designers

There are cover designers and then, there are cover designers. John has written several columns within his eNewsletter found at *www.BookMarket. com* on the topic (sign up). All of us agree that this is where a professional will shine and bring value to your book. If your cover looks amateur, it dominoes to what is perceived about the content. Not a good thing.

As with all professionals that you use, you need to check them out. Designers have different skills and preferences to working on certain covers. This is the time that you fully explore the designer's portfolio—don't forget the back cover as well. Pay attention to the use of graphics, font styles, any illustrations, color variations—are you wowed?

If the designer you engage doesn't produce something with a couple of passes that says that he or she gets your vision, he is the wrong fit for you and your book. Move on.

Back Covers Are as Essential as the Front!

Too many authors focus on the front cover and forget that the major sale comes from the back cover. Your front cover says pick me up, look at me ... and turn me over. It all happens in less than 10 seconds.

Next is the flip side. Your buyers spend more time on the back than the front cover of any book—your back cover could get a good 20 second look over. Does it have a bold "grab them" headline so they fall in? Does it pop in font size and color? It should lead the eye with tantalizing tidbits, facts, and copy that keeps the reader following your *piece de resistance*. How about three to five bullet points that are designed to hook the reader with "That's me; that's me … the author has written this just for me!" as your back cover is read. Add a paragraph or two about the book and hot dang … your book should be sold!

Don't get stuck on a bunch of endorsements—unless they are knock-your-socks-off with a name that is the guru in the genre you are writing in or someone who is gigantic in awe stature. The truth is, most endorsements are fillers and used when the copy in the body doesn't sing—you probably don't need them.

If you have a dust jacket or flaps, you get more real estate to pitch within. The inner front flap offers one more headline and more info that further draws the reader in. The next thing your potential buyer does is a quick look at the bio paragraph—do you know what you are talking about, have the credentials that support the topic? Include your photo—it doesn't have to be formal or stiff—maybe that one of you fly fishing last summer sends the perfect message that ties in with your book's theme.

And lastly, a quick thumbing through the book to look at the interior— is it presented in a readable format?

There's much more to a book than the front cover. When it comes to covers—the back, the front and flaps or a dust jackets—always think benefit to the reader. Your book shouldn't look like it was "self-published." Ever.

The Fundamentals of a Book Cover

There are key components on every cover—front, back and spine. They start with the:

Front Cover

Title: Does it say what the book is about in a glance? If there are graphics or cover photo(s), do they connect with the title/theme of the book? Make it big and bold!

Subtitle: Not all books need a subtitle. Not fiction. Use one if your main titles needs further explanation. Stay away from using key words in the title in the sub-title.

Illustrator's or Photographer's Name: If the contract with the artist requires it, you've got to do it. But, remember you are the author—your name goes first, and preferably bigger and bolder in font.

Cover Endorsement: Use one only if it's a major name—instant recognition for anyone that would be seeking your topic. Be wary of celebrities and politicians. They may be loved today and booed tomorrow—we want your book to be around for several seasons. If you have several endorsements, you can include them as front matter, which is placed before the title page.

Back Cover

Category Classification: All bookstores have departments and sections, be sure that your book is properly classified, by telling them where it belongs. Put it on the back cover, preferably on the top left.

ISBN: The 13 digit ISBN code is usually printed above the bar code on the lower left side.

Bar code: If you want to sell your book retail, you've got to have a bar code. Within it, will be the 13 digit ISBN code. It's normal to contain an embedded *price as well.*

Price: Even the price of the book is embedded in the bar code; you should put it on the back cover. Many also reflect a price for Canada. If you are going to include a reference to Canada, we suggest you use the wordage: *Price may vary in Canada.* That way, you don't have to worry about currency exchanges.

Author's Bio: This is not your resume—just include relevant bits and credentials which state why you are the expert to be writing this book. No more than a paragraph is needed—if you have a dust jacket or flaps, you can add more. A photo makes sense.

Headlines: The eye-grabber which makes a declaration; asks a question; makes a statement that leaves the reader dangling. In the newspaper and magazine worlds, there are people who just write headlines—that's their job. Pay attention to them; study them. What grabs you—pops out?

Synopsis: Think hook—what draws the reader in? What do you want him to "take-away when he reads your book? Your synopsis needs to be compelling and engaging—when it's read, the reader falls in. Just a paragraph or two.

Bullets and Callouts: Both add eye-candy to your cover. Bullets should be an odd number (three or five) and are written in a catchy manner to hook the reader. Callouts capture a major phrase, concept or even an endorsement that you want to pop—consider using a color that enhances the main background color.

Spine

Author Name: Sometimes first and last; sometimes just the last— your choice.

Book Title: Main title only; don't include the sub-title. Some authors print the title and their name vertically so they stand out on the bookshelf and can be read without the buyer tilting his head to read it. Most publishers print the title and author name horizontally. It's your call.

Publisher's Name or Imprint: Could be the name of the logo.

Bells and Whistles

Flat, blah looking covers don't have to be the norm ... and they are. Especially in the self and independent published realm. Kick it up.

Embossing, Spotkoting and a Bit of Foil

Think about embossing the title and your name. How about spotkoting a graphic or image, your photo or a callout box? Is there a color or a graphic within the cover that would lend itself to a foil treatment?

Printer's reps can be an excellent source to ask, "What if ...." They are much more than just quote getters for you. Think of them as a cover decorator—new methods and techniques come along each year that they can suggest after they see the initial design of the cover. They aren't your designer, they are your enhancer.

Gloss or Matte?

Most trade paper book covers are produced in a gloss, laminated format. Many believe the books hold up better and they like the shine that the gloss delivers. Maybe, maybe not. Judith has switched to a matte format for the books she personally publishes—she's found that the softer, non-glossy style "travels" better when she takes them on the road. This is a personal call on the author/publisher's part. Some printers don't offer a matte option.

Flaps for Trade Paper

One of Judith's favorite cover enhancements is the use of flaps—not only do they create more space for information about your book—but they look good. And, they create the feeling of a higher quality to the book. Which means you can charge a few extra dollars per book. Her imprint, Mile High Press, always includes the flap as a requirement for any book it publishes. Not all printers offer the flap option, you've got to ask up front. And, most book cover designers will charge a bit extra for their design work due to the extra associated with the cover design.

Yes, all of the extras aren't free, but they can make a huge difference in the eye appeal arena. Covers are about standing out—you want yours to be seen above the crowd.

Warning: there are less than 40 true book printers in the United States—those that print only books. We suggest you deal with printers who just print books. Each has different specialties. Some have a wide variety of options; others quiet limited. If you are calling all the shots, your can shop around. If you are working with a specific publisher, it may use only one printer, which in turn will limit what you can do.

Get yourself to a good sized book store and go cover window shopping. What pops out to you? Don't worry about genre here ... you are looking for covers that reach out to you—look at me, pick me up. What beckons? Study it and become a mimicker.

Whether you are pBook or eBook publishing, covers count.

Summing Up

When you talk with many authors who have published with the traditional New York type of publisher, it's not uncommon to hear grumblings about their book covers. They don't like the one their publisher created—colors, graphics, anything and everything. Each of us can tell you that there were times that we felt that our hands were totally tied in dealing with covers with our New York publishers. What we got was what they gave. The outcomes of many would win the prize for the most boring.

Covers can be, and should be, a work of art. They reflect what you have on the interior. They are a proxy for you, your siren to the buyer. The graphics, colors and design you choose are something you should be proud of. We want to give you ooohs and aaahs; not, "What were you thinking?" comments.

When it comes to covers, this is the place that you don't cut corners. Your book cover markets your book ... and you. Don't settle for anything that doesn't play, and say, your song.

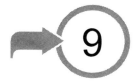

THE PUBLISHING
CLOCK IS TICKING ...
PRACTICAL TIMELINES

We confess ... here's one of our button pushers: book hustlers who tell you that you can publish over night ... or in a few days or weeks. Well, maybe you can get something out there—but it sure isn't going to be with bragging rights attached to it. And forget the award possibilities or kudos for a creative cover design. Your publishing success *will not happen* without planning. Books that look good, and are good, are not a "you too can write and publish your book in 30 days" event.

If you were to tell us that you need to have your book in hand because you have a conference that you are speaking at in October, we will tell you that your book manuscript needs to be edited, covers and interiors designed and layout completed, any endorsements obtained and approved, ISBN and Library of Congress numbers in hand and printer selected by mid-August. It gives some print fudge time and allows for shipping. A couple of months for offset printing—POD or a short run is much quicker.

Let's think out loud—most printers who are doing more than short runs will give a quote that will have books to you in four to six weeks—it gives them leeway and time for you to have one more time to proof the blue lines and return to them (Note to authors: making changes in the blue lines starts the cash register—most printers will charge $25 or so a page, and you go back to your interior designer to create a new PDF, which means she charges as well. You only make changes if they really need to be changed at this point.).

Assuming you want your publishing venture to have a good ending, it needs a good beginning. When you rush to print, mistakes are made. Don't.

Authors come in all kinds of sizes and shapes. Some are detailed and list makers; others may go with the spirit of the moment. Below you will find a laundry list of things to do—some need lots of time, some can be done in minutes (i.e., obtaining your ISBN). We are going to suggest timeframes within which to get them started, and completed.

Before you set up your roll-out time lines and you go to print, you need to consider whether you will seek endorsements and is your cover a wow. Thoughts on each:

> **Endorsements** If you want them, start early, long before printing is on your schedule. Endorsements should be from a recognized name within your genre that "like" readers will connect with. There are always exceptions, of course. If a major celeb or politician writes that your book is the best thing since sliced bread and that anyone would be a fool not to read it, this becomes a strong possibility.
>
> Unfortunately, too many authors use endorsements as fillers—they don't, or can't write good back copy so they hope that the endorsement will do the trick in intriguing a buyer. Rarely does an endorsement from your friend or uncle warrant printing on your book. If your friend is Diane Sawyer or Brian Williams—go for it. If it's politicians Nancy Pelosi, Sarah Palin or Harry Reid, you might want to thank them, but take a pass (or put it in the front manner within the book where a lot of publishers place the endorsements that aren't used on the covers). Why—because it's politics—people are very black and white and emotional in this area. Your book could be the perfect answer for what they are seeking, but seeing someone's name that they think is a total jerk endorsing it could lose the sale.

Our rule is to create great copy—if you get a worthy endorsement, terrific. If you don't, it's not a big deal. Breathe.

If you are seeking endorsements—ask what would work best—does the potential endorser want—a full manuscript, a few chapters, an abstract—what? Would a sampling of endorsements that have been pre-written be desired—he or she could select or rewrite or do their own (you would be amazed how many cherry-pick from the author's sampling of possible endorsements). Make it easy to work with you.

Covers Need to POP Using the right fonts, colors and graphics, a professional book designer makes a huge difference. This is prime book real estate. Front cover first, back cover second and if you have a dust jacket or flaps, third. Don't repeat the title of your book as the header on the back cover. Put your photo on the inner flap or the About the Author page.

It's wise to get extra covers. If you have a dust jacket, you can easily replace one that has been damaged. You may want to use them for promo purposes. And make sure you have an excellent digital copy of the front—you will be thankful when you discover how many places you upload it to.

Printing Depending on the method you print (digital or offset), there is a time factor. Digital printing is faster and, based on the printer selected and the number of books needed, can be within a couple of weeks. For offset printing, budget in four to six weeks for the process. If you require overseas printing, you've got to add a few more weeks for boat transit. Your printer will be experienced and have guidelines for you to final destination.

Depending upon when you need books in hand, your book must be completed, edited, and interiors and exteriors designed. Then, add the printing time. Now, drop that into your timeline.

4 – 12 months BEFORE your book is published, here's what to add to the authoring "to do" list:

You have finished writing. You have edited. Your cover is done. Sometime within this period, you will go to print. And, you will start:

Pre-Selling Your Book. Closer to four months out vs. twelve. Create the flyers mentioned in the chapter on *Pre-Publication Platforms*. Distribute them everywhere you go. Offer your book on your website, through your blog and any other medium you have. If you speak to groups, make sure you distribute them to everyone in the audience. If they like what they hear you say, even if on another topic, many will be inclined to preorder your book. Create a special deal for anyone who buys it before the publication date. By the way, our form of a deal is not to discount the retail price—we usually include shipping the book for free. Depending on what you are charging for shipping, that could amount to a 25 to 35 percent savings.

Thinking Promotion. Create a "sell" sheet, order sheet and start working on copy that will be used in catalogs. You need a bio (short). Start gathering names of publications that you can contact and send your sell sheet to for review and serial rights consideration. No one wants to read a bunch of "blah, blah, blah" soft stuff. Think ruthless editing as you prepare your promotional information. Once you get endorsements or reviews (or awards), you can pull a few lines and include them on a new "sell" sheet.

Thinking Media and Publicity. This is where Rick shines. As the founder of Planned Television Arts (*www.PlannedTVArts.com*), the leading book publicity firm in the country, he's seen every nuance in book publicity for 40 plus years. He's worked with every major publisher and author. Rick knows the tricks of the trade—it starts with a hook and a pitch. One tip he emphasizes is that all authors learn the use of the fill-in-the-blank formula. It starts with creating a show pitch that is guaranteed to grab a producer's attention virtually every time. Here it is:

Pitch Formula:

"You vs. _____ = _____ secrets to _____."

And here are a couple of examples of how you might apply it:

Pitch: "You vs. the IRS: 5 little known secrets to winning an audit."

Pitch: "You vs. your fear: 7 hidden secrets to crushing your inner demons."

Here's why it works: wherever there is *an opponent,* wherever there is a *battle or conflict,* people are intrigued. Period.

Identifying Bookstores and Events in Your Local Area. If you want to do author events at bookstores, identify which stores support authors, especially local authors. Gather the names of event managers, phones numbers and emails. Introduce yourself, let them know that you have a book coming and that you would like to do a signing and bring customers to their stores. When you send anything to a bookstore, follow-up. They get a lot of junk.

Sending Above the Author Crowd. Your branding comes into play. Whatever you mail—be it snail mail in a FedEx or UPS format, be a tad different. Most authors send their stuff in a brown or white box or envelope. Not you. Add some color—Bright red or purple or orange or … envelopes. Get some duck tape (it comes in every color under the sun) or some other tape and add some spiffy stripes to the package. When you follow-up, you can easily say, "Mine is the purple one … or has orange kangaroos on the front …." Be different. Be memorable.

Building Your Social Media Presence. Facebook, Blogging, Twitter and Podcasting will all be factors in the success of your book. If you aren't doing them, get ready … and started.

Purchasing the URL for *www.YourBookTitle.com* … and *www.YourName.com* … and *www.YourPublishingImprintName.com*. Make it easy for buyers and fans to find you. They may remember your name; the title of your book; even the name of the publisher. If the name of your book is taken, get the URL and just add "book" to the title—the odds are minimal that someone else has the dot com. All domains should be directed to one main one, the one that you keep current, which for many authors is their name.

Your website should have the ability for any visitor to buy your book … both pre launch and post publication. You can link buyers to B&N, Amazon or through you directly and pay via PayPal or another online payment merchant that you have set up. You can also include your order sheets that can be printed out and faxed, emailed or mailed to you.

Creating Your Website … Now. Yes indeed, you must have one. Start hunting and assessing websites to see what grabs you. Look at colors, fonts, graphics, styles, photos, videos, gadgets and gimmicks used, what's included on tabs and to click to. What do you like? What don't you like? A savvy website designer will always ask those two questions. Each of us has websites. Let's look:

Rick's is at *www.RickFrishman.com*. It opens—you see what Rick looks like, you can hear his voice, watch a video and read accolades. You can click to speaking, blog, publishing, bookstore, PR services, resources, other sites he's connected with, a blurb on his Author 101 University, etc. Rick's got a hot Rolodex feature to get tons of references; all obtained by submitting your email and a download comes your way. In a glance, you get a feel of what Rick is about. You may not choose Rick's colors (he likes blue), but it's Rick. And it's clear that Rick is connected with books and publicity and is a power house in the industry.

John's primary site is *www.BookMarket.com*. When you open it, you learn quickly that he's all about creating worldwide bestsellers and you see a photo of John speaking at a workshop. His thing is book marketing and book promotions and he's got multiple affiliates and websites. Accolades are led by Jack Canfield and how John was instrumental in creating the strategy that led to over 100 million copies of the various *Chicken Soup for the Soul* books being sold. There's a conference coming up that he presents around the country at *www.TenMillionEyeBalls.com,* reports available to purchase (we strongly suggest you get *Top 700 Independent Bookstores*) and he has his book cover of *1001 Ways to Market Your Book* prominently displayed. He recommends other books to support the writing and publishing journeys, has a Teleseminar Series that you can subscribe to and supports specific causes. You learn all this on the Home page ... and its primary color is blue too.

Judith's has three distinct sites. The first is *www.TheBookShepherd.com*. Along with her partner, Katherine Carol, she's created a book publishing consulting/coaching practice that caters to the author. When you visit it, you will find photos, live video, white paper to download, newsletter, blog, featured authors that she's worked with, authors who are in the news or are celebrating an event around their books, information about how she works with clients, speaking, etc. You can find the latest issue of *The Resource*, an author and publisher newsletter on the site.

Other sites include *www.Briles.com,* which is dedicated for speaking for associations and groups, primarily health care. It's designed for meeting planners of events that bring in speakers—speaker information, introductions, kudos, calendar, topics, blog, bookstore, etc. Her other site is *www.AuthorU.org,* a membership site of authors that has a newsletter, blog, click to join, resources, calendar of events, regular author and publishing related BootCamps, members in the news, etc. Each are different, yet there is a connection—with Judith, her passions and with her favorite colors, purple and green, part of her branding she started as a speaker 30 years ago. Blue isn't her thing.

Where your website is built is important. We think that you should have immediate access to it; to be able to add articles and tweak once in awhile without incurring the National Debt. One of our favorite platforms is WordPress. Yes, the blog format.

Setting Up a Merchant Account. You have to take credit cards if you want to sell books. No exceptions. Start with your local bank and determine their rates. QuickBooks (*www.Intuit.com* or 888-335-4541) has a program that has no set-up or application fees. There will be monthly fees. If you are a member of IBPA, the International Book Publishers Association, you have access to its merchant status program (*www.IBPA-online.org*). Options change frequently. Crunch your numbers to determine which program is best for you.

Getting Setup with RR Bowker. You want to submit your book information for inclusion in *Books in Print (www.Bowker.com)* with their ABI (Advance Book Information) form. If a buyer is in a book store and asks them for your book, the odds are that it's not in inventory. The first thing the employee does is go online to see if it's in the store/chain's inventory and next up is *Books in Print*—can it be ordered. And, of course, you want them to be able to find you and order it for the customer. This is how to do it.

Identifying Publications within Your Niche. Do they feature books? Authors? Call or email (info will be on the editorial masthead) and determine what the lead time is as well as who to send your book to. Besides groups that you are already familiar with, there just might be hundreds, even thousands more. The National Trade and Professional Associations Directory (*www.ColumbiaBooks.com*) is available at your public library lists them by categories, states, financial size, contact info and even whether they have a publication—you name it. A significant amount of information is at your fingertips; information that opens up an avenue you haven't thought about—not to mention information about conferences, conventions and budgets (meaning—paid speakers or not).

Identifying Publications to which You Want to Send Review Copies. Consumer magazines come and consumer magazines go. Not all publications are going to want your type of book. Your job is to figure out which are the right fit. The Internet is a terrific resource.

Don't forgot associations and niche groups—thousands of them create newsletters and internal magazines that are worthy of your attention. You may have never heard of them, but they've got a loyal following/membership who read what the group produces.

If it's your niche, you want to be in it.

Make contact first to determine if there is an interest—you don't want to kiss off unnecessary money by putting together an expensive presentation coupled with your book and have it go in the trash.

Some reviewers want to see the book or a galley several months prior to publication *(Publishers Weekly, Library Journal); others* prefer the book in post publication *(MidWest Book Reviews).* The wise author makes a few phone calls and makes sure that she submits per the publication's guidelines. Some will list on their websites; others, you've got to call and clarify.

Creating Media Releases: Regular Mail and eMail Formats. Producers and editors use email aggressively. So should you. For email, keep it short and sweet. Give them pertinent info, leading with a hook that they can handle in less than 30 seconds. The less, the better. Create a grabber subject line for attention. Media pro Alex Carroll routinely sends out ideas on how to grab producer's attentions. Sign up for his free newsletter at *www.RadioPublicity.com.* Rick Frishman sends out media ideas every Sunday night. You can sign up at *www.RickFrishman. com* to receive his ideas, plus a variety of other leads for promotion. Make sure your contact and information is in the signature of the email. DO NOT SEND ATTACHMENTS. Not until you are asked for something. No exceptions.

The same concept can be used for the longer, mail version. If you've ever seen a media release—contact info is at the top with publisher name, along with title and often the cover of the book. Sometimes, the publication info is included (ISBN, page count, price). The verbiage— multiple paragraphs about key concepts, usually some bullet points and sometimes the author is cited.

Creating an eMail Signature. Your name, email, website, possibly a key slogan that you are identified with and of course: Author of the forthcoming book (your book title). When the book is in print, then shift to Author of (your book title). You can even include your photo and the front cover of book when you have it. Use it always. We are always amazed that so many authors miss the boat on this one.

Speaking … Think Speaking. Depending on your topic and which groups would be attracted to it, you need to be reaching out. When is your annual meeting? Or next? Do you bring in speakers? Who decides on which speakers and programs? How much planning time is needed? Include as part of your fee, the ability to sell your books. Take credit cards, checks and cash. If you are comfortable, sometimes an IOU and then bill immediately (if you do this, add a note on the invoice that if items are not paid for in 15 days, there will be a late charge and state what it is). It's smart to be there an hour before your speaking time and scope the site out.

Ask your host if the attendees are a book buying group. You will sell more books in the day vs. the evening time. Bring books for about a third of the crowd. If it's local, always carry a few cases in your car.

If you are speaking at an event whose participants come from a general area, contact their local bookstore. Let it know that you are speaking, possibly doing media and would like to be able to refer buyers to their store. If you have a distributor, let it know your calendar as well.

Connecting with a Wholesaler or Distributor. If You Want to Sell Books in a Bookstore, You Need a Wholesaler or Distributor. There's a difference. The wholesaler won't be pitching your book for you; it will, though, send books to a bookstore if requested by it. Think of a wholesaler as a warehouse. The distributor is much more. Part warehouse, but also pitcher to bookstores and sometimes key media. If you are planning events that put you in a specific regional or anything on a national basis, keep your distributor in the loop. It can alert its sales team to get books there in time.

Authors learn quickly—books are impulse buys. If they aren't there when the buyer wants them, something else may get their fancy.

Creating an Amazon Account … Amazon Is Amazon. The biggest online store in the sky and one that you need visibility within. Some authors grumble that they take a huge discount. Our response … so? It's a bookstore; bookstores buy at discount to resell at a retail price. End of story, get over it. Self and independent publishing will continue to morph. Amazon's Advantage program is still the main one. Set up an account and start loading info including your cover art (make sure you pay attention to the format it specifies). At this printing, all can be found at *www.Amazon.com/Advantage*.

If you do any type of publicity, Amazon is a must vehicle for you. A buyer can do a hunt and peck with key works, including your last name or a portion of the title, until they find your book.

Creating an Amazon Bestseller Campaigns. Should you or shouldn't you? The answer is: it depends. They take time. You need to put work into it; build a wide network of supporters who will in turn contact everyone in their database to direct them to go to Amazon on a specific day to buy your book. Usually whoever is in on the campaign offers a special deal/give-away to any buyer. There are lots of email reminders that have to be generated, and of course, no guarantees. The critical element is having the right team that will start the word spreading and recommendation that their "crowd" buys your book.

4 Months Pre-Publication ... Your Clock Time is Shortening

It's time to tighten up the year. With four months to go until "official" launching, here's where you are:

- **Start Thinking Flyers, Postcards and Bookmarks.** For postcards, put the cover of your book on one side; on the other, include your photo and return address at the top. Write something catchy in the body—give the recipient some "action" to do—order your book—call you about speaking. You may want to make two or three cards—one for buying the book; one for speaking; and one for thank-yous—you only need just your photo and return address, leaving you with a few inches to write a note. Not only does your addressee see the book cover, so do all the hands your post card has traveled through.

- **Mail Out Review Copies** to groups that you have determined require three to four months in advance of publication. When you receive them, file them. You will use in promotional material; add to your website; or if one is "hot", you may want to get it on the final cover, or add to the front matter of the book. Both of these are "ifs"—If you have already printed, you have printed. Save for the second round.

- **Connect with Local Groups to Speak to.** Many locals plan the calendar as much as a year out. Most don't pay. No matter. Offer to "waive" your speaking fee in lieu of being able to present on your book and having it available for sale. Depending on the group, and its size, you could ask that everyone gets one included with their register (the host buys from you or a bookstore for the number signed up). Or, you could simply have them available.

- **Author Tours Are an Option.** In the old days, publishers planned on touring their front list authors to key cities. That's not the norm today, unless you are a celebrity of some sort. You can, though, create your own tour, and why not?

If you've got the money, then the sky is the limit. Most authors don't. The frugal way is to piggyback events and activities already planned for (i.e. the family reunion in Chicago in May; the high school reunion in San Francisco in July; or your sister's daughter's wedding in February). If you are going to already be there, expand your time and presence. If you have points in air and hotel programs, this could be ideal for using them. Minimal moneys go out the door.

You then reach out to the media—radio, TV, even print. You are an author. You will be in town on the days of _____ and ….. do *your pitch*. The local Chamber of Commerce has a list of groups that meet regularly. Get it by calling—most will gladly email it to you. Are there any during the time you can be there? Call and pitch yourself and your book. Is there a bookstore? Call it. Can you do a signing (and get all your high school pals to come out and buy, buy, buy)?

Judith has done extensive author tours. Some arranged by her New York publishers; some created by her. How did she get on *Oprah*? She pitched it directly. Featured in *People magazine?* Ditto. On *CNN, CNBC,* in the *Wall Street Journal?* Ditto. Ditto. Ditto.

She learned that once she perfected her pitch, her hook and who to call, no one could do it better.

You can hire someone to pitch you; but you better be able to pitch yourself in the first place.

- **If Anyone Owes You a Favor or Thinks You Are the Cat's Meow, Ask Him to Host a Signing.** Why not?—Jim Hall, author of *Parachuting for Gold in Old Mexico*, had worked closely in several political campaigns in Colorado. As Jim's book got closer to publication, former Governor Bill Owens offered to host a book signing. It was glorious and over 240 copies of Jim's book went out the door at full price. Enough to cover the cost of his first print run. That's a friend. Friends don't expect free books, they buy them.

- **Book Clubs Are Your Friends ... Catalogs, Too.** Contact book clubs and find out what their submission requirements are. In Chapter 14, *Mistakes to Avoid,* several book club websites are identified. You can also do your own Google search. Book clubs don't pay a lot of money for a book when they buy it; but, you should be able to negotiate a price over your actual cost per book. The good news is that your book is featured in a book club (this is a big congrats from us); books are paid for, usually within 45 days; and there are no returns. Some will allow you to purchase their member/mailing lists.

- **Publicly Calendar Your Events.** Speaking, book signings, awards, etc. Carry them on your website. The Google calendar can drop in easily on your site. Announce them in your newsletters. Do this at a minimum on a monthly basis. Don't bombard your email recipients with too much, but stay connected ... the celebration is coming!

- **It's Photo Time ... Yours.** If you don't have a photo (you want both color and black and white), this is the time to get it. Author photos don't have to be created in a studio. Some of our favorites are casual—a friend has caught the author in just the right mood, pose or place. Or the author is doing something he loves—fishing, skiing, racing (probably not best to be tipping a beer). It's okay to show some personality. John often uses one of him casually speaking; Rick has one that has him in a casual pose; and Judith's was taken on a cruise ship by her daughter. All cropped, all work for them. Do what works for you, but get them and make sure you have 300 dpi versions. All should be available on your website along with your media release.

- **Post Your Media Release on Your Website ... and Start Releasing It.** For the next several months, including post publication, you will be sending this to people. The media, groups interested in hiring you ... anyone. Yes, they can easily download it themselves. But you are going to find that you are the captain here. You may be on the phone and telling the person on the other end that the information they are looking for is in his email as you speak. Always make it easy.

- **Set Up Speaking.** And do it on an ongoing basis from now on. Your new attitude is *Got Book ... Will Talk.*

- **Pay Attention to Your Local Media.** Is there anything hot going on that pertains to the subject of your book? Has a reporter written anything that you think is terrific—and it doesn't have to be about your topic? This is a great time to get those postcards out and drop a note and let her know that you enjoyed her feature—keep up the good work. It's connection building time. You are going to do this on an ongoing basis as well.

- **Pre-Pub Selling.** Add this to your ongoing list. Everywhere you go, your birthing book is available for purchase. Carry your flyers. You've made them, now use them.

3 Months Pre-Publication ... Tick Tock, Tick Tock

- Books Are Coming. You want to have books in hand a few months out from your official launch.

- Continue to send advanced copies to publications, groups and individuals that need time three months out.

- Keep honing your pitch.

- If you haven't planned a special event to kick-off your book launch, this is the time.
- Don't forget commenting on blogs—yours and others.

2 Months Pre-Publication ... Tick Tock

- Connect with reporters and editors at newspapers. If appropriate, remember to tie it into something that might be hot in the news.
- If you are sending out a book, you want it to be the finished product, not a galley.
- Create media releases around scheduled appearances that have been made—do timed releases so more than one is sent out.
- Reconfirm your radio and TV contacts.
- Revisit your media package—the one-sheet, your website (do all the links work?), your packaging—anything that you are sending out. Is it top notch or second thought?
- Whatever you send out, you must schedule yourself to do a follow-up call a week later.
- Continue to add to your website any reviews, kudos and events. Don't forget your own blog. Social media takes time, but when it comes to books, amazing things can happen.
- Create the rollout of an eBook along with the printed copy of your book. Buyers like choices. There are a variety of sources to assist here—we like *www.DarkFireProductions.com*. You can create an eBook for $50 for all the major eBook publishing platforms.

1 Month Pre-Publication ... Tick

- Whatever your didn't get done, this is crash time. Tie up the loose ends.
- Whatever media contacts you had identified on a shorter leash, this would be the time to send info out to them.
- Update your one-sheet.
- Prepare and mail out postcard blitz to radio, TV, newspapers.

- Send postcards to your local bookstores.

- Blitz Internet radio sites you've identified. Remember, keep this short; use a snappy subject line in your email outreach.

- Follow-up with local and key media—did they get your info; is there interest; remember your Pitch.

- Use social media to keep your buzz going.

- This is a hectic month—if you have been a solo act the last few months, you might want to engage a virtual assistant to help with your launch.

Book Publication Day ... Tock!

Yes, you should celebrate. It's your choice, you choose how. You may be on a plane starting your tour. You may have a key interview slated. You may have a special party planned. Whatever it is that you have opted to do, it's a huge bravo coming your way!

PRE-PUBLICATION
PLATFORMS ...
SELL BEFORE YOU PRINT

Ahhh, the lure of publishing can be very seductive. Most people feel they have a book in them and yearn to get it out. We love the idea ... but love it far more if you've got a plan on how to launch your publishing passion and succeed in selling books—lots of them.

Truth be told, this is where most authors fail miserably. They've got big ideas. They can see their book; hear their readers say bravo; even see money coming their way. They just didn't see, hear, feel or create the way to make that happen.

In the Beginning

Launching your book requires pre-publishing work. You want your book's audience to know you, who you are, be connected with you, trust you, and, look forward to your printed words. *You start the process before your book is available.*

The Internet is a comrade in the process—you can start the buzz all by yourself. Twitter, blogging, ezine articles—there are multiple formats to use. In print, you can start writing articles for publication in newsletters, magazines, even newspapers. Always, with the tag that you are the author of the forthcoming book your comments are based on. And, of course, reference to your website (where they can find information about your book and pre-ordering a copy).

Start with:

1. *Knowing your book*, which is often easier said than done. Be able to verbally ID your hot selling tips (you are the primary salesperson—never forget it); the top five benefits why someone should own your book; who your audience is; what's the single biggest issue that they are dealing with (around your book); and the number one take-away that your book delivers.

2. *Create five to ten informational* and how to articles for *www.EzineArticles. com* or *www.HubPages.com.* These high-traffic sites have thousands of visitors on a daily basis. Offer free eBooks, additional articles, white papers, special reports, a newsletter and don't forget to mention your Twitter and Facebook addresses or any YouTube segments you have.

    If you are submitting to multiple sites, make sure you have a "variation" on the theme. Otherwise, you may run afoul of Google's Duplicate Content rule—basically when someone submits the exact same thing over and over with the objective to advance positioning within the search engine—and earn the Duplicate Content Penalty—go ahead, Google it and learn all about it!

    If they read your article and visit your site, they are in your camp—a very good thing.

3. *Get a jumpstart* on your book sales by pre-selling your book before you have it in hand. Make it easy to buy your book. Create the ability to pre-buy it at a special price. Include shipping (which could be the special price—charge the regular price of the book for the pre-sale with the free shipping as a bonus). Wherever you are, have a flyer that a buyer can complete and give you back a check, cash or include their credit card info. On your website, have info and a link that allows them to buy now.

    Be a little vague—instead of saying "Available September 15, 2011," go with "Available Fall 2011"—you now have three months to get it out. A three month window is so much better than one day.

4. *Create a pre-publication flyer or form;* include the book cover if you have it—otherwise go with the title; use bullets to ID benefits—talk to your potential buyer; and a brief bio on you. We have used a discount of 20 to 30 percent ... it's mostly shipping. If the book will retail for $25, pre-sell it at $25 net—if shipping was added, it would be another $6 or $31—the buyer saves 20 percent ... and gets a personalized copy from you when you send it.

5. *You need a website, now.* If you already have one, create a promo for your book—right on the Home page. Add a splashy, get-the-visitor's-attention button and link. It can lead the visitor further in with greater detail. If you have testimonials from known names, highlight them. Make sure you use bullets with key benefits. As the reader peruses them, our goal is to have the reader "sold" by the third bullet point. Be careful, and wary, of long sales pitches—your visitors may become un-visitors.

6. *If you are website shopping,* don't make it complicated. Word Press (the blog creators) has become the norm for many websites today. Why—fairly easy to use, and you—the author—can easily make changes without having to pay a bunch of bucks for a webmaster to update every great idea you come up with. You, literally, become the master of your domain.

7. *Tell the world.* Let your Internet surfing and clicking do your walking. Social media becomes one of your best friends. Twitter, blog, Facebook, LinkedIn are all powerful resources to get your word out. Use them wisely.

8. *Twitter is growing like topsy.* Share tips and expertise with your fans (even if they haven't found you yet). Link Twitter, Facebook, LinkedIn, your blog and any other social media you are using by using *www.Hootsuite.com* ... one entry is posted everywhere.

9. *Visit other's blogs.* Make comments on blogs that are related to your topic or field. The higher the traffic the blog is, the more visual attention you get. You may be asked to do a guest blog.

10. *Create a list of how-to tips* that are of course, from your book. Distribute through your blog, Twitter and Facebook.

11. *If you see a current event* or item in the media that you can connect to, reach out with a media release format—a great lead-in on the problem/issue, how your book can solve it—catchy bullets and your contact info.

12. *Speak.* If you aren't already speaking about your book to target groups, start now. With audiences, books are impulse buys. When your book is still in process, having a pre-publication-special flyer that everyone in the audience will receive can create sales. If they like you and what you have to say, many will fill them out.

When you have book in hand, you will still be doing most of our list above. Pre-publication-specials will disappear; you won't be mentioning "forthcoming" in your tag line; and you will have books at all the talks and presentations you do. You are a published author.

 Getting ready for your book's launching is a lot of work. Remember, this is a new business you are moving into. It will take time, money and work. When you know who your audience is, you are able to narrow your message to fit their needs. The more you niche yourself, the bigger your audience can become.

Creating a quality book that engages your audiences will translate to sales. Your goal. The buzz factor via word of mouth will increase them. Having a website that is inviting, easy to navigate and offers information keeps people coming back. And, reaching out and using social media strategically lands you on our honor roll list.

If you build it, they will come.

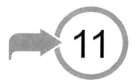

FOREIGN RIGHTS ... WHERE YOUR MAILBOX FINDS A FRIEND

Your book is property—intellectual property that you can sell the rights for others to use. One of the most common, and too often overlooked, is in the area of foreign rights. Just because you don't speak or read Chinese or Arabic shouldn't be the deal stopper in going down this avenue.

Our gifts aren't in the ability to initiate a face-to-face discussion with someone fluent in a language outside of English. We are, though, quite skilled in page-to-page interaction with the written word. Our books have been published in multiple countries and languages throughout the world. Each time a contract is entered into, a check arrives in the mailbox.

Getting a foreign rights deal usually happens with the use of a publishing agent who is connected in a country. It means they will get a percent of the deal, which is usually 10 percent. They handle the paperwork on your behalf and the foreign publisher steps to the plate and bear all the costs involved in getting your work translated and published in its country.

The publisher states in the contract whether it will be publishing and distributing your book in either English in English speaking countries, or translating it into a foreign language in non-English speaking countries. It's wise to pay attention to which countries are included in the publisher's "umbrella"—you could overlap another deal you've already committed to.

Also note the timeframe of the contract; when the publisher must publish your book by; and how royalties are paid. If the publisher doesn't get the book published within the stated contract time, you are now open to resell your book to another publisher that handles rights for that country. Before you do so, it's smart to formally, in writing, notify the publisher that the contract has terminated. If you worked with an agent, copy him with all correspondence.

Getting Your Book to Travel

Here's how it usually works: Your goal is to license your work—the book—to a foreign country that in turns pay you for that right to publish, market and distribute it. You get paid in the form of an advance (usually not huge, but it's money and can sometimes amount to several thousand dollars). If it sells well, you could get additional royalties. More money. Think of it as diversifying your assets—in this case, your book.

Traditional publishers usually have a connection to an agent who specializes in foreign rights. Which is a smart thing—different contacts, languages and negotiating. For the self and independent publishers, you can Google and Bing contact possibilities or connect with an agent yourself to represent your work. If you do, you will find that most will attend the Frankfurt International Book Fair in the fall and possibly London's. Some may also attend the BookExpo of America—Frankfurt, though, is the biggie. With the rapidly shrinking BookExpo, Frankfurt's attendance exceeds both London and America by thirty fold.

 If you choose one to have your book represented, just leverage yourself and put your money at Frankfurt. People come from all over the world just to buy foreign rights—hundreds of thousands of them.

If a foreign publisher or agent wants to preview your book, send it. We know, there's always the fear that they could take it and print it anyway—but that's part of the business person's risk (Judith knows this dance, it happened to her in France without her knowledge, much less permission—and certainly no thank you letters with a check included!

How did she discover it—simply by Googling her name in Europe and one of her book titles popped up).

It could take a few weeks or several months before you know if an offer will be made on your book—one that could be a few hundred or many thousands of dollars.

When a request is made for a review copy, make sure you have a cover letter that IDs the book, the author, the publisher, the ISBN, address, email, and phone number. In most cases, send it by using an International Priority Mail envelop—your cost will be in the $11 area and will arrive within a week to its destination. Plus, you can track it, which is a good idea.

What Are They Looking For?

Ahhh, the $64,000 question—what books sell in foreign countries? The answer is that books that have "legs"—they can travel and don't carry "restrictions"—meaning tons of references to too many things that are American. Think taxes, locations, schools, institutions, people and places. Now, Bill Clinton's book did quite well globally—but it was all about Bill and of course had his name on it as the author—that's different.

John's book, *1001 Ways to Market Your Book,* is universal in its appeal. Authors are everywhere. They want to know how to market their books. He offers loads of advice, how-tos and websites to go to. Being in China or India isn't a huge concern—tips on marketing and selling have a global language to them. Judith has several books that have had multiple sales in a variety of countries. Business books, how-to books, psychology based books. Her books that she wrote on personal finance aren't successful in foreign markets—simply because American strategies and taxes are the wrong hooks. Rick's books on obtaining publicity, positioning and PR also have a global flavor to them—what works in America could be the cat's meow in India, with just a bit of a twist.

Foreign publishers are looking for what's a fit for their country, their readers. It's that simple. What are the common connectors? Think business, self-help, entrepreneurship, how-to, and psychology. They are on the constant lookout for the new twist or angle. Fiction is a tougher sell.

Size counts. If your book has become a tome—lots of pages, foreign markets backpedal. Of course, Bill Clinton's memoir fit that category, but he was, well, Bill Clinton—it didn't matter. Business books that are in the 200 to 250 page count in English do far better than the 450 page latest offering.

Why so? Think translation. Throughout Europe, a 250 page book morphs into a 340 page baby. That means there is more money outgoing to production—costs: printing, paper and shipping. In Asian based countries, it's the opposite. Your 250 page masterpiece drops to 175 pages.

What Happens When an Offer is Made

A contract comes your way. You will be asked to send a specific number of books to the agent representing the foreign publisher, the publisher directly or another party designated by the publisher. They may request electronic files. Make sure you have both snail mail and email contacts for both the publisher and their agent. Why? There's always follow up, including getting a copy of sales ... which means you could have royalties coming your way. After contracts have been signed, you will get a check in the currency you've requested. And, congratulations!

Who Wants Your Book?

Books will probably have roots for a long time in the foreign markets. Yes, the Internet is everywhere. And yes, eBooks are growing in popularity—yet they represent less than 10 percent of book sales. In foreign countries, the pass-around rate for a book is huge; much less probability of passing one's computer amongst friends to read the latest chapter or book.

Over 400 countries have publishers. Within those ranks, the number swells to the tens of thousands mark. As of this writing, the countries that appear to be the most aggressive in seeking books include China, Thailand, Korea, Indonesia, Japan, India and most of eastern Europe. More sales are coming from Spanish speaking countries. One of Judith's favorite covers comes from Saudi Arabia for her book, *The Confidence Factor*—her name is in English, of course, the rest is Arabic with a huge golden egg.

It's important to say here that your book does not have to be hot off the press to get foreign attention. Maybe you hadn't thought that the Chinese might embrace your savvy formula for fast-tracking a new business when you published it five years ago; or entrepreneurs in India were chomping at the bit to get your strategy for marketing products; or that your book on rebuilding confidence would be sought out in Croatia. Your ideas, your words just may be ready for the rest of the world, now.

Have Book? Start Connecting Today

We like to think of foreign rights money as found money. It's a great day when those checks find their way to your mailbox—a new friend. Below are some samples of websites that you can start the connection process directly. There are also agents in America who have connections with agents in foreign countries. Each will take a piece of the money pie.

Here's a partial list of several agencies that represent foreign rights. Some of the addresses will take you directly to the contact list; for others, you will need to click on a tab or put "foreign agents" in their search window.

www.SwayzeAgency.com	Canada
www.OBrien.ie	Ireland
www.Escritores.org/recursos/agentes	Spanish
www.Esslinger-verlag.de/foreign/agenes.php	German
www.McClelland.com/rights	Multiple countries
www.RandomHouse.ca/rights	Multiple countries
www.ScribePub.com.au/rights	Multiple countries
www.TLA1.com	Canada, UK, Europe
www.Temple.edu/tempess/foreign_rights.hml	Multiple countries
www.NewMarketPress.com/foreignrights.asp	Multiple countries

www.Loewe-Verlag.de/rights/agencies.html   Multiple countries
www.SpectrumLiteracyAgency.com/foreign.htm   Multiple countries
www.Bob-Erdmann.com/foreign-rights.html   Multiple countries

A book can die, or go into a coma, prematurely. Bookstores may deem the timeframe for a book to find an audience is equivalent to the length of time a Chinese meal sticks with you. Meaning, not long. If it's run its course in the bookstores, you as the author, and publisher, need to come up with a strategy to stretch its life. Or find new ones.

Implementing a foreign rights strategy is one way to expand your book—your financial asset. Your cost will be minimal to pursue it, which makes it a plus. As with anything, it will most likely not happen overnight. You will have some misses and rejects. What doesn't work for one publisher's list, will work for another's. What doesn't work this year may be the perfect "got to have" book for the next year. Being committed to a program usually brings positive results. A return on your investment. And, money in your mailbox.

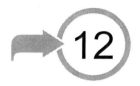

REBOUNDING WHEN
YOU HIT THE WALL ...
EVERYONE GETS
STUCK SOMETIME

Somewhere along the publishing process, you are going to hit the wall. Roadblocks, detours and screw-ups are going to get in your path. One of the most common is the naïvete factor. Most first time authors think that when their book is written ... they are done. Dream on. Your book is a manuscript and in a draft form. It's a lump of coal waiting to be polished to become the diamond you envision.

You've had friends read it; and friends tell you that it rocks. But does it? Unless it's had a good round of editing, it's not ready to rock or roll.

Books take time. Each step breeds another. What you do need is that *Plan* we've mentioned throughout *Show Me About Book Publishing*. There are components: creating the manuscript; editing; designing interior and exteriors; printing options; creating your infrastructure to support sales and drive sales to a buying point; and marketing strategies within and outside of the Internet.

Plans are roadmaps. In publishing, your Plan is your guide through the processes and maze you are undertaking—and it is a big undertaking.

Too many authors rush to publish, truly believing that they've created a masterpiece, when gulp, sometimes it looks and feels a tad like Frankenbookstein.

All processes have a pre, during and post cycle. Your book is no different.

Let's start with the Pre-Book Phase.

If you haven't finished your book yet, reach out. Don't be shy. Too many authors develop a paranoia that someone is going to steal their idea and beat them to the punch. How long did it take you to get to this point? A few months? Years?

Do you really think that someone you know is going to read your manuscript and turn around and publish it at the drop of a dime? And, especially for nonfiction, do you truly believe that you, and only you, have come up with your concept? Highly unlikely. Similar ideas, concepts and plots are floating everywhere.

It's a smart author who gets input from others. Often, it's good and can open up new ideas and twists you hadn't thought of. Ask for suggestions on how to make your words, plots, or concepts more powerful.

The best time to bring an editor on board is before you finish. You'll find out quickly if you need help in the developmental area, with plotting or dialogue early on.

Depending on where you live, the odds are that there is a robust and healthy writing community within the genre that you are working in. Writers and authors are terrific supporters for new and experienced authors. Don't go it alone, especially in this stage.

You've got a completed manuscript ... what's next looks at the *Got Book Phase.*

This is the "look in the mirror" time for you. So, what's it going to be—a few copies for the family, a select gathering of friends or a specific group or association you are a member of? Or are you planning on selling it at a retail price ... and if so, to whom? Book stores? Libraries? Private groups? At speaking gigs? Where ... and better yet, how? Or, is your dream to sell it to New York?

This is where a book shepherd or publishing consultant can be invaluable. Money will be an issue. Who and what your platform is will be another. Time lines come into play as well as control issues. If your goal is to sell it to New York, you don't care about ISBNs, fulfillment obligations, finding printers and designers ... or, should you?

We think that the savvy author thinks seriously about how she wants her book to look, and to feel. That means openings of chapters; font selections; covers—back and front; decisions about hardback vs. trade paper; whether illustrations will be used, etc. Even if your intent is to sell your completed manuscript, the wise author should be fully prepared to let a publisher know what her "vision" is for how the book looks and feels.

If you are bypassing traditional publishing, which mode will you select? Is it the bare bones option where you contract with someone to drop your work into one of the templates and cover options that the POD publisher offers that requires minimal upfront moneys from you? Or will you stretch to the other end of the spectrum and get ready to announce the birth of your own publishing imprint?

Choosing the latter means your have plenty of prep work. From obtaining ISBNs, applying for your Library of Congress number to making sure you have the right team in place to create your piece of publishing history, and creating a website where hungry buyers can purchase your book (even before it's officially in print).

When your book is in hand, it's all about the *Birthing the Book Phase ...* also known as *The Work Your Tush Off Phase.*

You've done it; it's in your hands ... now what's next? Social media, social media, social media. Facebook should be your fan. Create a Fan page and start gathering them. Are you on LinkedIn? How about creating a group? What about the Blog universe? Have you checked out the top blogs in your genre? Are you subscribing to them; making comments if allowed and appropriate where they tie into your book? Have you considered offering to do a guest blog for your favorites? What about Twitter? You could have a Twitter account around your name as well as your book or topic. It's a whole new fan base.

Create your own eNewsletter and submit articles to ezines and other resources on the Internet that welcomes content. Is your book listed on Amazon *(www.Amazon.com/Advantage)* and Barnes & Noble online *(www.BN.com)* and have you created an Author Profile page on Amazon?

How about creating a webinar around the principles of your book, even charging for it *(www.TheWebinarMentor.com)* or design a workshop or speech that incorporates your book? The book itself could be required reading by every participant in a workshop, so it's included in the workshop price (nice!). When speaking, you would make your books available for purchase by attendees, usually at full retail. After all, you have lugged them to the site and are personalizing them.

We strongly recommend—no we insist—take credit cards, at least Visa and MasterCard. Discover card is also fine; just don't make it the only card you accept. American Express is another option, but not as important as taking Visa and MasterCard.

You will find that your book and product sales will double when you allow for cashless purchases. Always make it easy for the buyer to buy. Accept credit cards. Along with cash, checks and when appropriate, invoicing for groups and individuals within a group. If you are speaking at a function that's in a gaming environment, go ahead and take chips but restrict them to the hotel/casino that you are speaking in so you can exchange them onsite.

If you are selling to a company or group that has employees, ask about employee payroll deductions—forms are filled out by the employee that are supplied by the group, and the group does all the paperwork and collection of money. You should get a check within 30 days—just make sure you have a detailed list of who bought and what they owe before you leave.

How you choose to launch your finished book is always a venture. Traditional publishers select a month first, date second. Judith has always recommended to her clients that the Rolling Launch model be embraced. Sure, pick a month, even a day within in ... but that's the starting point; not something that is going to end within a few weeks as the traditional publishers practice. Take an entire year to "launch" your book ... it's your journey. Make it a party!

This is a major part of the *Working Your Tush Off Phase*. You didn't write this book overnight; why should you execute the launching in an overnight fashion? Start it, nourish it, let it blossom and grow. Your book could easily tie into various media twists throughout its life. Watch, listen and respond to opportunities as they arise.

Are you going to pursue media opportunities? Hire a publicist? Is it going to be more traditionally based, i.e., TV, radio, print media or Internet/social media based? Or a combo? There are book publicists out there who specialize in each.

We have to throw a big caution sign out here: *PR and media can be your money pit*. There are no guarantees that bookings will be successful; or if there are bookings, that you and your book come off as brilliantly as you thought you would and the hoped-for-sales get generated.

This is a good time to be marketing and media smart. Get your name, your thoughts and views out there via the Internet: the free approach. A few of the blogs, Twitter accounts, eNewsletters (all free) we recommend you follow to get your feet wet before you start spending money include

John Kremer	*www.BookMarket.com*	*Twitter.com/JohnKremer*
Rick Frishman	*www.RickFrishman.com*	*Twitter.com/RickFrishman*
Dan Poynter	*www.ParaPublishing.com*	*Twitter.com/ParaPoynters*
Penny Sansevieri	*www.aMarketingExpert.com*	*Twitter.com/BookGal*
Joan Stewart	*www.PublicityHound.comj*	*Twitter.com/PublicityHound*
Dan Janal	*www.PRLeads.com*	*Twitter.com/PRLeads*

Alex Carroll	www.RadioExpert.com	
Judith Briles	www.TheBookShepherd.com	Twitter.com/MyBookShepherd
	www.AuthorU.org	

Zigging and zagging are part of the writing and publishing path. Wouldn't we all love to wake up one morning and declare, "Yep, there's a book in me and I'm ready to write it. Nothing will prevent me from getting it done …"?

Life happens. An accident, a new romance, kids needing your attention, work, divorce, summertime … you name it. It happens. There are going to be diversions along the path. Some you will create; others will be a roll of the dice. *Those zigs and zags may just turn out to be the most direct route you could have taken.*

Book publishing is not an overnight proposition. We know of no authors, including us, who haven't had a few hiccups along the way. Getting stuck can last a few days, weeks, sometimes months. Part of your Plan should include "what to do" to get your rebound in motion when needed.

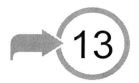

YOU THINK YOU ARE DONE …
YOU ARE NOT

Your manuscript is both good and original; but the part that's good isn't original, and the part that's original isn't good.

Samuel Johnson

Wahoo! You think you are ready to publish your book … yes, but … most authors, turned publisher, think that writing the book is the toughest part. Hmmm … maybe, maybe not. We think your real work is just beginning. Let's go down the book journey path you are ready to embark upon, are in the middle of, or just completed.

In the Beginning …

Creating the book.

You know why *you are the author* for this book and *who the reader* is.

Hopefully, you didn't wake up one day and say, "I know, I'll write a book … now, what should I write about … maybe someone will give me a hint."

As the author, you are the expert—what brings you to the party? Successful authors have passion—passion erupts from involvement. What sets you—and the book you've written—apart from other authors who write within your genre and field?

One of the things that always amazes us is the belief of many authors that their book is for "everyone." Hogwash. Even a book that sells in the millions has millions that can't stand the topic, subject or even your style of writing. It happens.

It is the rare book that makes it to the *New York Times* bestseller list. Books published by traditional publishers normally sell well below 10,000 copies; most likely below 5,000. That's not much money to you as the author—if you are lucky, you might make minimum wage.

Better yet, to ID your niche—know *who* your reader is … then find them. There are a variety of ways to target your specific audience, drill down and sell to it. It's where savvy marketing comes into play. Drill, author, drill.

You researched it.

You determined what your unique angle/twist is and can now state it in one sentence … Yes?

For nonfiction, what research did you do to support your topic, theme or position? Did you do any interviews to support your work; are there case studies? And most important, are they interesting, supportive or controversial—did they move your position and work forward?

For fiction, is your story line interesting, or has it been told a zillion times before? Boiler plate like? Are your characters unique, quirky, people that the reader wants to connect with, get info from, avoid like the plague, endearing—what?

You don't want to create someone or a scenario where unbelievable, dysfunctional or darkness is out of character/tone with the theme of your book. Or, that there isn't one redeeming value, nor any connection, where the disappointed reader tosses the book aside—usually within the first 25 pages.

You planned it.

Let's review: every book has a beginning, a middle and an end. Fiction, nonfiction, children's, even poetry, all have structure. Did you select the right beginning? The middle, supporting cast or building of the story? How about the end—is there a solid conclusion, a good "aha," wow or take-away? Or satisfaction that the story delivered the punch, release or pleasure it intended?

You didn't jump the gun by writing too soon.

You may have a terrific idea, but did you do yourself, and your reader, a favor by not rushing to write too soon. Or publish. Sure, it makes sense to start compiling notes and ideas—but they are the beginning, not the end.

Ideas take time to jell. It's amazing how one path can lead to a detour that may offer the perfect solution, bridging or add depth you hadn't originally conceived. Rushing may lead you astray in the process, not allowing you to maximize your offerings to your reader.

In the middle ...

Once you starting writing, you took your research cap off.

You did your pre-work—didn't waste time doing more research when you started writing. For nonfiction and fiction, it doesn't mean that you didn't pay attention to any late breaking stats or research. And it doesn't mean that you didn't add some phrases or techniques that new techno gadgets introduced during your writing that added flavor to your idea or storyline.

We don't want you to get caught in a "one for the money, two for the show, three to get ready, three to get ready, three to get ready—you won't go. You have to say, "I've got enough to create my book." Get going. Start writing and putting your puzzle masterpiece together.

When you've completed the first draft, step away.

It's a good thing. You need a mental, and physical, break. Read something for total pleasure. When Judith finishes the first draft of her next book, her "reward" is to take a week off and ready trashy novels—anything that isn't in the business arena and preferably some type of suspense thriller.

Go play. The bonus is that your "break" often clears out the congestion that intensity can bring—and new ideas surface. You don't want to write in perpetuity—that's what your next book is all about. It's a good thing to take a break.

In the end ...

Mini vacation is over ... it's time to revisit your manuscript and make mini notes as you do a fast read.

You are fresh ... think content, don't focus on punctuation here. Does your book flow? Think of yourself as the buyer and reader. Does it grab you and flow? Do you like it?

You've got margins—use them, make notes for those "ahas" that will come to you when you take a few days away. You are looking for redundancy, blah and boring passages. Things that you overlooked, because you were so immersed in your manuscript, surface after a break from it.

For nonfiction, if you haven't supplied "eye breaks" with headings and callouts, let your eye be your guide. For key points, bullets, boxes and shadings are eye helpful. For fiction, is your story moving forward—have you used a "show the reader style" vs. a "tell me" style?

Are your openings as sharp as you want; do your segways and transitions flow to each new chapter? Is your ending as appealing as your opening?

Do one last read through before submitting to your editor.

Note the typos (they will still surface); count on it after you've been through it a zillion times. Be ruthless. If you've got phrases, sentences, paragraphs that aren't critical to the chapter, delete them. Does it invite you in? Still make sense? Can you close it and say, "That's a great book or story."?

Before you have books in print, pre-sell them.

Savvy authors learn that pre-sales pay bills. You get sales by asking for them. Create a flyer; offer a discount if the book is bought before publication date. Include shipping as a bonus. When you determine what your costs are per book (editing, design, printing, shipping, consultants), you know just how many books you need to sell to cover your costs at the reduced rate. The more of your books you can sell that will generate revenues, the happier your checkbook will be.

Get ready for your next book.

Books can procreate. It's amazing how one idea seeds another. Be ready to collect comments from readers, they could just be the genesis of what's next. Has anything new surfaced in your field? Anything you wished you had included? Is there anything in your book that has popped—could one of your chapters morph into a separate book? Did any "ahas" come to you after you completed it.

Roll your sleeves up.

You are going to print—what about the supporting cast?

Does your website champion your book? Does it have your name or your book title as the URL? Does it look professional? Websites are about information and branding. This is not the time to be cutesy or clever. Your readers need to find you without needing a PhD in cleverness. Blog and Twitter info should be apparent on the Home page. Is it easy to navigate? Include a free chapter or two for a look-see and how to buy.

Don't make the mistake of making your website the only place to buy your book. You need the online giants as partners, the ability for the brick and mortar stores to get inventory (meaning you need a wholesale or distributor relationship), and we would strongly encourage you to have both audio and eBook formats. The more the better.

Gather names—as many emails as you can.

From the get-go, you want to start the gathering process. If for some reason, this became a hiccup along your authoring path, kick it into high gear. Collect emails via your website. Any list that is generated where people have "opted in" is gravy for you—you've already built some rapport and trust.

Use a service such as Constant Contact, to create an attractive newsletter that will land on your website (and visitors can sign up for). Keep them informed of the progress of your book, even the few roadblocks you've hit. Share your breakthroughs and celebrations. By the time you go to print, you will have a cheering section rooting for you. And ready to buy.

 Publishing is an amazing journey, loaded with unbelievable zigzags and paths. In the end, they just may be the most direct route to getting your book completed. If you strive to create the "perfect" book, your journey may not end. Perfection is the enemy of the good ... and your book could just be the next great thing!

MISTAKES TO AVOID ...
OR SAVING MONEY 101

There isn't an author we don't know who doesn't have a list that starts with "Next time ..." An author and publishing bucket list of things to do "right" vs. snafus and boo-boos along the way. Mistakes cost you money. Sometimes small; unfortunately, sometimes enough that it could knock you out of the playing field.

Here are some of ours:

Not Doing Your Pre-Work

If you haven't done your pre-work to know what's out there in the bookstores and on the Internet, you are making a huge mistake. If you don't have your name, your topic, key phrases registered on GoogleAlerts, you get demerits.

Bookstores, and the people who work in them, can be an asset. For the developing author, experienced bookstore employees can offer some coaching—what's moving in the store; what colors are popping on covers; what type of books customers are asking for; or what types of problems are customers seeking solutions to?

Pay attention to what's happening within your genre. Whether it's in the news; in the blogs; or in your head, be prepared to tweak when needed. What you don't want to create is something that has become passé.

Authors need platforms. They need to identify where their crowd is. The Internet can be a huge factor. With a few strokes, your may find a viral world that is chomping at the bit for your info. If you already have a following, you should be teasing them with "glimpses" of what's to come.

Savvy authors not only let their crowd know that a book is in the works—they start the buzz; and, they begin to take orders before it's printed. Orders can be taken through your website (yes, you have one or will before your book comes out) or create a flyer that you can distribute wherever you are. When people pre-pay, those funds should be used to offset your production costs.

Not Creating Deals

Deals can be done before a book comes out, or after it's in print. Make special offers. Pre-selling allows you to test the market response, your potential cover and the price.

If you think you are going to price your book at $20, offer it to early buyers at $20 and include shipping as a freebie. That's like getting a 25 to 30 percent discount if the buyer had to pay full retail plus shipping. Any resistance allows for tweaking—including the change in price. And, if there is no resistance to the $20, consider notching the price up a few bucks the next time you put your flyer out. Judith raised the price of her book, *Money Smarts for Turbulent Times* from $15 to $20 to $25 over a three month period of speaking to groups where she distributed a pre-publication flyer she created.

Pre-sell to groups that know you. If you are a speaker, distribute flyers everywhere you present; if you have an Internet following, tell your fans your news—you've got a book coming and because they are your fans or clients, they can order a copy at a special discount and receive it before others.

Your book may tie into a company or a product that would make it an ideal candidate for sponsorship or being used as a premium. These things rarely fall into your lap; you need to seek out and pursue.

Not Offering Pre-Publication and Post Publishing Flyers

Timing is important. We suggest that you don't sell more than six months prior to availability. And don't tell the buyer that the book will be shipped on a specific date unless you know that it is a guaranteed date on your part. Let's face it—things happen that could delay a book. Be they rewrites, interior or exterior design, editing, printing ... or just maybe you've lagged a tad. A little breathing room helps. Instead of saying that your book will be available September 15th, better to say Fall—that gives you a three month window.

If you have settled on the price, offer your special at that price with the free shipping as the incentive. That's going to give the buyer a decent discount. Let the buyer pay by cash, check or credit card. Process everything and don't spend the money unless it's for the printing. That way you know that you will have a book to mail to the buyer.

After your book is printed, create a form or flyer that is included with all book shipments. Why? To—

- Remind the buyer that your book can be ordered, personalized, directly from you;

- Ask the buyer to go to Amazon and post a terrific review (lots of potential buyers read them)—you want as many 5-Star Reviews as possible!

- Offer deals/discounts for multiple purchases.

Not Speaking

When others love your book, or discover that it delivers a solution to a problem ... your voice is golden—use it. And get paid for it. Pay comes in for form of a speaking fee; it also comes in book sales. Better yet, a combo. Should you speak and not get paid—maybe.

Judith has spoken professionally for three decades, meaning she gets paid when she opens her mouth. Ninety percent of all her presentations have a speaking fee attached to them. The other 10 percent? Marketing and caring—her approach is that if she believes that there is someone in the audience that can hire her at her speaking fee, she will do it. Or, if she feels passionate and is dedicated to the group, she will waive her fee. Otherwise, she is paid and her books are sold at the event.

National groups can engage you as a speaker, so can local. There may be book clubs; there could be groups that in lieu of paying you, everyone buys a book; there could be groups that bring you in and include a copy of your book in the registration fee.

 Always have your book with you and *always* carry a few cases in your car. You are in sales now.

Not Pitching to Book Clubs

Book clubs don't pay top dollar, but they buy books (at a deep discount), pay you and don't return them. There are general interest, lifestyle, special interest and professional clubs. The *www.Book-Clubs-Resource.com* site is an eye-opener for general information on clubs, reading groups, how to set one up and online options. Let the Internet do the walking for you—here's a few you should explore:

- *www.Book-Clubs-Resource.com*
- *www.BookClubDeals.com*
- *www.BookSpan.com*
- *www.BooksOnline.com*
- *www.AllBookClubs.com*

As an author, you need to be into book promotion, book marketing, book publishing, self- publishing, selling your books, selling e-books, POD publishing, Internet marketing, print-on-demand, website promotions, or promoting a novel—and you want information and resources to help you sell books—our eNewsletters are up your alley.

Sign up:

- *www.BookMarket.com*
- *www.RickFrishman.com*
- *www.TheBookShepherd.com*
- *www.AuthorU.org*

and Twitter and Facebook accounts at:

- *www.Twitter.com/JohnKremer*
  www.Facbook.com/JohnKremer
- *www.Twitter.com/RickFrishman*
  www.Facbook.com/RickFrishman
- *www.Twitter.com/JudithBriles*
  www.Facbook.com/AuthorU
- *www.Twitter.com/MyBookShepherd*
  www.Facbook.com/TheBookShepherd

Not Using a Professional Editor

The difference between most self-published books and small, independent and traditional publishing can be summed up in one word: editing ... or the lack of it. If your book is loaded with errors, the odds are that you've lost the reader.

Not all editors are the same. Ones that do copy editing (grammar and typos) may not be the same as editors who are content and developmental editors. Content and developmental editors are word doctors. Their goal is to make your words, phrases and ideas pop. And, don't forget, editing flows to your cover and dust jacket copy as well.

Not Using the Right Cover and Interior Designer

Covers are the Barker to the reader and buyer. Your book shouldn't look like it was self-published, ever. Covers are a critical investment in the presentation of your book ... not just the front, but the back. Where the front is designed to say what the book is about and conveys, "Pick me up now," it's the back cover that should get them to fall in.

Buyers spend more time on the back—does it have a bold "grab em" headline? Headlines shouldn't be a repeat of the book title—this is your second sell. For nonfiction, are there three to five bullet points that are designed to hook the reader with "That's me, That's me," as they read through them? A paragraph or two about the book and they should be sold. Period. Don't get stuck on a bunch of endorsements—unless they are knock-your-socks-off and a major voice in your genre, you probably don't need them. Always think benefit to the reader.

If there are more books in you that are related to the topic, think series and start your branding—with your image, logo, phrases, colors, title and your name.

Not Engaging the Right Printer

Each of us has a great time with our printers … at least with their reps. They know how we want our books to look, feel, know the print runs we normally use. The relationships that we have are like the ones that a banker used to have with his depositors (note—we said "used to"—with ATM banking, bankers are clueless as to who you are). Our printers know us and our books. Does yours?

We recommend when you are searching for a printer, that you:

- Get a minimum of three bids for 1,000-2,000-3,000 (unless you have pre-sales that scream to get thousands and thousands, stay with under 3,000). You will note that there is a true price break once you go over 1,000.

- Make sure that printer is in the book printing business— there's a big difference between laying out brochures and laying out books.

- Get references.

- Ask for samples or books that have been printed that are similar to what you think your specs are.

- If you are using interior color, use a printer that specializes in color.

- Understand the difference between digital and offset printing.

As *Show Me About Book Publishing* is being published, there are only 39 book printers in North America!

Not Branding Yourself as the Expert

As the author, you are the expert. Wear it proudly and position yourself. You do it with your book; any presentations you make; with interviews and the media. Your expertise is integrated with your brand. Phrases, key/buzz words, designs, colors, affiliations all become part of your persona.

Branding is used within your book, on the covers (front and back), in your marketing material—everywhere. Branding is about you.

Lynn Hellerstein is an optometrist who specializes in vision therapy. She is the author of *See It. Say It. Do It,* a book all about using visualization to achieve goals. It's presented as a tool that is highly interactive for parents to use to help their kids in areas like sports, math, music, reading, dealing with homework and tests. Using strong primary colors, a banner with the title was created that is woven throughout everything she does—her website, webinars she gives, media releases, articles, programs she presents—you name it; once you see it, you recognize it instantly.

When she started winning book awards, she tapped into the title and added, *See It. Say It. Do It! Did It!* When she sees a news item involving kids and sports, academics or music, she would reach out to the media source and offer her input as an expert.

Not Having a Written Plan

The plan is to have a plan. You can hire out or you can do yourself. Your plan acts as a guide to what your book is about; who your market is; how you are going to reach out and connect with it; what media support you are going to use; how much money you are going to invest in your venture; even, what kind of spin-offs you are thinking of. Not having a plan is a good way to practice the art of floundering.

Not Doing Targeted Media/PR Marketing

If there ever was a giant sucking sound in publishing, this is the arena that usually gets the most votes. Mega thousands of dollars can be kissed off in the area of PR.

Most people, and certainly authors, would assume that if a program/ plan was created, moneys committed to it, that there would be success. Maybe, maybe not.

In PR and publicity, authors and publishers quickly learn that there are no guarantees. You may be scheduled to do a segment on a coveted program and get bumped at the last minute because of a late breaking news (i.e., Paris Hilton was arrested!). We know, your info is more important ... but producers have quirks of what "they" think is important. Paris, or whoever the celebrity of the week is, is in ... you are expendable. You are "out."

And you, or the person you hire to rep you, could pound the media circuit and pitch ... and get zero results. You have to ask: Did your PR rep do a crummy job? Is there no interest in your topic? Is your information material, including media release or hook mediocre? Is there major news that is bumping everything? What?

What we do know is that it's critical to be focused and targeted. PR and no-guarantees go hand-in-hand. The more that the author steps up to the plate to assist in the orchestrating of the campaign—even pitching it—the more success can come your way. And, it's important to understand that "traditional" media—such as pitching to national television or radio, may not be the right fit.

What does your crowd—your book buyer—watch or listen to?

- PR and media should be directed in avenues where there are buyers for your book.
- Use a list of top book buying cities (Minneapolis, Seattle, St. Paul, St. Louis, San Francisco, Los Angeles, New York, Denver, Portland, Atlanta, Boston, Dallas, Atlanta and Washington, DC).

- Media and PR are basic to sales ... sell the benefit to the listeners, viewers and readers.

Oprah isn't for everyone. There are, though, hundreds of other venues that are the perfect fit for your topic.

Not Using Social Media to Market Your Book

Yes, you will most likely do some publicity and PR. But, both have taken a back seat in the book buzz world to social media—primarily, Twitter, Facebook and LinkedIn. The next book in the *Show Me About* series will be all about using social media to market you, and your book. You will need to create a Facebook page along with a Fan page, start Tweeting (no, not what you had for breakfast) and get involved with groups on LinkedIn. Social media is all about finding your crowd, community, or "tribe" as author Seth Godin refers to it. And communicating with it on an ongoing basis.

Not Treating Authorship and Publishing as a Business

Are you in this for "something to do" or are you serious about being a success? Be clear on what it takes to break even—just how many books do you have to sell to cover your initial expenses? Do you have a plan? It's your choice, you choose. Reread Chapter 3, *Money Talks ... Do You Listen?*

Not Cutting People Who Don't Work with and for You

Be loyal to your book and your vision ... don't let others tell you what you think; seduce you in going down a path that doesn't feel right; or spending/costing you moneys that you don't have.

Not Seeking Out Independent Book Stores

We know that Barnes & Noble is the gorilla of the major book stores. It's great to get your book into the chain, but consider the independents—much easier to get your book on their shelves and create a signing. Here's a list of some of our favorites:

Seattle WA	Elliott Bay Book Store
Portland OR	Powell's Book Store

Denver CO	Tattered Cover Book Store
San Francisco CA	City Lights Books
Menlo Park CA	Kepler's Books and Magazines
Los Angeles CA	Dutton's Books
New York NY	McNally Robinson Booksellers (also in Canada)
Austin TX	BookPeople
Dallas TX	Half-Price Books
Houston TX	Brazos Bookstore and Bookstop
Minneapolis MN	Wild Rampus and Magers & Quinn Booksellers
St. Paul, MN	Birchbark *Books*
Atlanta GA	Atlanta Book Exchange and A Cappella Books
Washington DC	Politics and Prose Bookstore and Coffeehouse
Boston MA	Tatnuck Bookseller & Café and Brookline Booksmith

Not Staying Visible

Don't assume book buyers are going to find you ... you have to go to "them," don't wait for the phone to ring. Brand everything you do and become the expert in your marketplace; use GoogleAlerts; follow Blogs and Twitter accounts and make comments when appropriate; write articles that tie in with your book and place them on the Internet as well as in newsletters and magazines that your "crowd" reads or has a membership with; and, be generous—don't be afraid to use your book as a calling card ... meaning that you give it to people that you know who will spread the word (or hire you to speak).

By the time you've got your book in your hands, you will have your own list of "Note to self: next time, don't do this ..." We know the journey, compiling our own lists along the way. You will make mistakes, we all do. The key is to learn, and not repeat.

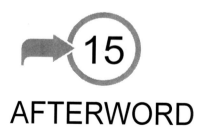

AFTERWORD

Whew ... what a journey this thing called publishing is. At this point, your eyes may feel bleary, your body is screaming for another option of activity and your brain ... well, your brain might be telling you it's overloaded.

And we have to tell you the journey is just beginning. But what a journey you are on. Publishing is a theme park of surprises. At times, you will have your arms in the air, shouting to any and all that you've done it; at others, you experience the darkness of a tunneled ride just waiting for the next thing to spook you.

We are excited that we can be part of your ride, your journey. Each of us has taken it several times. And guaranteed, there were times that we wanted to toss the towel in and find the nearest exit. Each time, the Publishing Siren beckoned, luring us back.

Being hooked on publishing creates a river of new friends and contacts. You will meet people, gather fans that you never imagined would hang on to each word and idea you created and have a rocking good time. Send us a postcard, a tweet or an email along your way.

John, Rick and Judith

RESOURCES, RESOURCES & MORE RESOURCES

Updated rolodex at www.rickfrishman.com

If there's something that the publishing field has lots of, it's Resources. When exploring your options, get references ... and let the Internet guide you with problems. We recommend that you put in the name of company or individual in Google and follow it with "problems," "complaints" and/or "scams" and see what pops up. You would be amazed what you can uncover with a few clicks.

If you have concerns, complaints or just want to check something/someone out, here are a few sources to guide you:

- The Author's Guild, *www.AuthorsGuild.org* is one resource;

- Another was created by the Science Fiction and Fantasy Writers of America, *www.SFWA.org/beware*;

- Whispers and Warnings can be found at *www.WritersWeekly.com;* and

- Don't forget just Googling a publisher, vendor or supplier's name and put "complaints," "scams," "warning," or "problems" after the name. If there are alerts and grumblings, they will surface.

And if, unfortunately, you've stumbled across someone who has created problems, a warning from you might just be appropriate.

Space doesn't allow us to list them all, but here are some that warrant your attention:

Book & Author Organizations & Associations

American Booksellers Association (ABA)
www.BookWeb.org
Book trade association of approximately 4,000 retail booksellers. ABA sponsors the IndieBound program, which brings together booksellers, readers, independent retailers and local business alliances.

American Library Association (ALA)
www.ALA.org
The official organization for all libraries. ALA has more than 65,000 members and holds annual and regional mid-winter meetings.

American Society of Indexers (ASI)
www.ASIndexing.org
ASI is the only professional organization in the United States devoted solely to the advancement of indexing, abstracting, and database building.

American Society of Journalists and Authors (ASJA)
www.ASJA.org
Non-fiction organization of a 1,000 plus members nationwide. ASJA maintains the *Freelance Writer Search* that lists writers, editors and project managers for hire.

Association for Christian Retail (CBA)
www.CBAonline.org
Previously the Christian Booksellers Association, CBA is a trade association whose members create and distribute Christian books and products.

Association of American Publishers (AAP), Inc.
www.Publishers.org
Membership trade organization of the publishing industry. Nonmembers can attend the *Annual Meeting for Small and Independent Publishers*. AAP offers programs for small and independent presses that cover a variety of author and publisher strategies.

The Authors Guild
www.AuthorsGuild.org
Membership organization that represents thousands of published writers and authors.

Author U (university)
www.AuthorU.org
Membership organization that has monthly meetings, BootCamps, member only newsletter and discounts to a variety of publishing suppliers.

Book Industry Study Group, Inc. (BISG)
www.BISG.org
Individuals and firms interested in promoting and supporting publishing industry research. The keeper of book categories.

Independent Book Publishers Association (IBPA)
www.IBPA-online.org
Formerly Publishers Marketing Association, IBPA is a membership organization specializing in small and independent presses and self-publishers. It holds its annual Publishing University each year just prior to BookExpo.

Note: IBPA has Affiliates or Sister Organizations that represent regional organizations consisting of self and independent publishers, such as the Arizona Book Publishing Association (*www.AZBookPub.com*), Author U (niversity) in Colorado (*www.AuthorU.org*), Bay Area Independent Publishers Association (*www.BAIPA.net),* and the Small Publishers, Artists, Writers Network (*www.SPAWN.org).*

National Speakers Association (NSA)
www.NSASpeaker.org
An association of professional speakers that offers excellent conferences and networking opportunities. Authors should learn to speak on their books. Check your local state for group closest to you.

Poets & Writers, Inc.
www.PW.org
Publishes several reference guides and subsidizes readings and workshops.

R.R. Bowker
www.Bowker.com
The exclusive U.S. ISBN and SAN Agency, Bowker receives the most authoritative title and publisher information available. Books in Print updates at *www.Bowkerlink.com.*

Small Publishers Association of North America (SPAN)
www.SPANnet.org
Members consist of authors, self-publishers and independent presses.

Speaker Net News
www.SpeakerNetNews.com
Tips for professional speakers online.

Writer's Digest Books
www.WritersDigest.com
Publisher of *Writer's Market* and other books useful to writers.

Writers Market
www.WritersMarket.com
Database—over 6,000 listings—that can help both writing and publishing that's updated daily. From magazine submissions, to finding the perfect person to create a postcard, use this site. There is a nominal membership fee.

Publishing & Government Services (including forms)

Library of Congress
www.LOC.gov

Library of Congress Copyright Office
www.Copyright.gov
http://www.LOC.gov/loc/infopub/
http://www.LOC.gov/copyright/forms/

Library of Congress PCN Program
http://PCN.loc.gov/
http://PCN.loc.gov/pcn/pcn007.html
http://ECIP.loc.gov/pls/ecip/pub_signon?system=pcn

LOC Cataloging in Publication Data Program
http://CIP.loc.gov/cip/

Copyright Clearance Center
www.Copyright.com

Copyright-Term
http://www.Copyright.Cornell.edu/training/Hirtle_Public_Domain.htm
www.Copyright.Cornell.edu

Publisher's in Cataloging-in-Publication Request Form
http://www.DGIInc.com/pcipform.htm

Patent & Trademark Office
www.USPTO.gov

Legal, Intellectual Property, Copyright, Trademark Attorneys

Tonya M. Evans
www.LegalWritePublications.com

Steve Replin
www.ReplinRhodes.com

Lloyd Rich
www.PubLaw.com

Brenda Speer
www.BLSpeer.com

Jon Tandler
www.IR-Law.com

Book Shepherding, Coaching & Author Services

Animations
www.AnimationFactory.com
Animations for presentations including PowerPoint.

Andrew Chapman Media
Andrew Chapman
www.AChapman.com
Over 20 years experience providing professional publishing services for print, digital, audio, and video

Tom Antion
www.Antion.com
Strategies for Internet Marketing and Speaking Butt Bootcamp.

The Book Shepherd
Judith Briles & Katherine Carol
www.TheBookShepherd.com
Our motto: Create, Strategize, Develop, Publish and Achieve. Crafting and publishing a book with no regrets is no small feat—we do it with all our clients; even the ones we have to rescue! Coaching and connecting you with excellent editing, interior design, distribution, and marketing, and marketing strategies for PR and social media.

Cartoons and Illustrations
Shannon Parish
http://shannonparish.com/brochures/cartoons.htm
Get your message across *instantly* with cartoons and humorous illustrations. Viral marketing, book illustrations, workbooks, presentations, products, educational materials and more!

Cartoons, Illustrations, Websites
Don Sidle
www.DonSidle.com
Your one stop shopping for just about any type of cartoon, graphics, logo, drawing, website. Finds a creative solution to graphic dilemmas.

Clip Art
www.ClipArt.com
Over 10,000,000 downloads at your fingertips. You can access the entire site for a month and download to your heart's content for less than $35—and use in your book.

Rick Frishman

www.RickFrishman.com

Will counsel you on all types of media and marketing. Rick works with several media companies and can help you.

From Passion to Publicity: *Getting Your Book the Attention it Deserves*

Lin A. Lacombe

www.FromPassionToPublicity.net

Provides strategy, messaging, publicity and various book development, promotion and How-To packages for the independent author and/or publisher.

Sheryn Hara

Book Publishers Network

www.BookPublishersNetwork.com

Expert group of publishing professionals with 20 years of experience dedicated to providing the superior book production hundreds of published authors know and trust.

Haven Books Consulting

Reya Patton

www.HavenBooksConsulting.com

Author Services: Book Coaching from a professional award-winning team including editorial, book design, web design, publication set-up, distribution & fulfillment set-up, marketing plan.

Brian Jud

www.BookMarketing.com

Book marketing, TV promotion, special sales expert. His *How to Make Real Money Selling Books* is a must-have for any author. Free newsletter, sign up on website.

John Kremer

www.BookMarket.com

Book marketing and promotion consulting—Author of *1001 Ways to Market Your Books*—sign up for weekly marketing tips through website.

Logical Expressions, Inc.
Susan Daffron
www.LogicalExpressions.com
Book interior layout, cover design and publishing consulting;
specializing in working with small independent and self-publishers who
print through Lightning Source.

Marin Bookworks – The Book Designer
Joel Friedlander
www.TheBookDesigner.com
Services for publishers and authors including design, layout and
production.

Market Savvy Book Editing
Chris Roerden
http://WritersInfo.info
Highest-quality book editing of nonfiction and mystery.

Peggy McColl
www.Destinies.com
Works with authors to create products; build global branding; online
launching strategies with Amazon and BN; and Internet marketing.

McNaughton & Gunn/Westcom Associates
Michael Vezo
www.Help-U-Publish.com
Complete Author and Publishing Services.

Dan Poynter, ParaPublishing
www.ParaPublishing.com
The go-to site for all things related to self publishing. Get his book,
Self Publishing Manual. Free newsletter, sign up on website.

PeopleSpeak
Sharon Goldinger
www.DetailsPlease.com/peoplespeak
Book shepherding and packaging services with an eye for details,
covering editing, design, production, distribution, marketing and
publicity.

Premium Book Company

Brian Jud

www.PremiumBookCompany.com

Commission-based sales of books to non-retail, non-bookstore buyers.

Ellen Reid Book Shepherding

www.Smarketing.com

Positions and works with authors on their books; from manuscript to print and website.

The Technical Writing Company

Barry Schoenborn

www.WVSWrite.com

Publishing services that help publishers and authors take care of the important processes that must be done to get a book "out the door." Advise about improving procedures, or just do the tasks for you.

Three Pyramids Publishing / publishing and technical writing services

John Simone

www.Three-Pyramids.com

Established in 1989, supplies complete technical writing resources, along with book packaging services.

Virtual Reference Desk

www.RefDesk.com

Fact checker for the Internet.

WESType Publishing Services

Ronnie Moore

WESType@comcast.net

Award-winning interior designs with over 30 years of experience in book layout.

Note: There are a variety of organizations and associations that cater to the writer and author. You can usually find them by Googling a key word, add "association" or "group" then a city. In Colorado, there's BOOC— Book Organizations of Colorado, *www.ColoradoBook.org*. Under its umbrella are a variety of specific groups—children's, mystery, you name it.

Selected Book Printers

Included are book printers, including POD. For more extensive listings and information, look in *LMP*. Always, always get references and check out quality. Some United States, Canada and Asian printers are represented.

ADI Books/King Printing
www.KingPrinting.com

Bang Printing
www.BangPrinting.com

Bookmasters, Inc.
www.BookMasters.com

Central Plains Book Manufacturing
www.CentralPlainsBook.com

Color House Graphics, Inc.
www.ColorHouseGraphics.com

DarkFire Productions, Inc.
www.DarkFireProductions.com (ebooks)

Note: Adobe's Content Server protects e-books in a PDF format from being traded/exchanged with other readers who haven't anted up for their copies.

Edwards Brothers, Inc.
www.EdwardsBrothers.com

Fidlar Doubleday
www.FidlarDoubleday.com

Four Colour Print Group
www.FourColour.com

Friesens Corp.
www.Friesens.com

Lightning Source
www.LightningSource.com

Malloy
www.Malloy.com

McNaughton & Gunn, Inc.
www.BookPrinters.com

Sheridan Books, Inc.
www.SheridanBooks.com

Thomson-Shore
www.ThomsonShore.com

Total Printing.Systems
www.TPS1.com

Websites and SEO

Here Next Year
www.HereNextYear.com Marty Dickinson
A veteran in websites, Marty Dickinson and his team have been designing them for over a dozen years for authors and companies.

Findability Group
www.FindabilityGroup.com Heather Lutze
You may have a website, but does the world know who you are and how to find you? The Findability team shows how with *The Findability Formula* (John Wiley & Sons).

American Author Websites
www.AmericanAuthor.com Lars Clausen
Offers powerful, affordable, and easy to use websites, specifically designed for authors.

Where to Send Galley Copies

People change—the wise author and publisher calls before placing anything in the mail. Determine who the contact is and make sure you get the correct name spelling. Many websites have detailed submission guidelines—check them out.

Booklist
American Library Association, 50 E. Huron St., Chicago, IL 60611-2795, (800) 545-2433, *www.ALA.org.* Submission guidelines found under Booklist.

ForeWord Magazine
Review Editor, 129. E. Front St., Traverse City, MI 49684, (231) 933-3699, *www.ForewordMagazine.com.* Submission guidelines on website. Reviews independent publishers.

BlueInk Reviews
Patricia Moosbrugger, 5910 S. University Blvd, C-18, #181, Greenwood Village, CO 80121,303-698-0116. *www.BlueInkReviews.com.* Reviews specifically for self-published books. Can send finished books as well.

Kirkus Reviews
www.KirkusReviews.com. Submission guidelines on website.

Library Journal
Book Review Editor, 160 Varrick, 11th floor, New York, NY 10013, *www.LibraryJournal.com.* Submission guidelines on website.

Los Angeles Times Book Review
202 W. First St., Los Angeles, CA 90012, (800) 252-9141, *www.LATimes.com/features/books.* Send one copy with a cover letter.

The New York Review of Books
435 Hudson St., Suite 300, New York, NY 10014, (212) 757-8070, *www.NYBooks.com.* See Website for submission instructions.

The New York Times Book Review
620 Eighth Ave., 5th Floor, New York, NY 10018, *www.nytimes.com/pages/books.* Submission guidelines on website.

Publishers Weekly
www.PublishersWeekly.com. Submission guidelines on website.

Quill & Quire

Quill & Quire, P.O. Box 819, Markham, Ontario L3P 8A2, 800-757-6177, *www.QuillAndQuire.com.* Canadian published books *only.* Submission guidelines on website.

School Library Journal

360 Park Ave. S., New York, NY 10010, 646-746-6759, *www.SchoolLibraryJournal.com.* See Web site for submission guidelines.

Where to Send Finished Books

Baker & Taylor Company

Publisher Contact Section, P.O. Box 6885, Bridgewater, NJ 08807-0885, *www.BTOL.com.* Submission guidelines on website.

Choice

The Association of College and Research Libraries, 50 E. Huron St., Chicago, IL 60611-2795. 800-545-2433, *www.ALA.org/acrl.* Academic publication—only send finished bound books. Phone to receive a copy of submission guidelines.

H.W. Wilson Company

Attn: Indexing Services, 950 University Ave., Bronx, NY 10452, 800-367-6700, *www.HWWilson.com.* Send one copy; the service will contact you by mail. HW Wilson has 42 journals (including *Book Review Digest*) at the website.

Selected Cities

Always include your local and regional newspaper book review editors and cities that you've had a connection with/to. Don't overlook sections within the newspaper. If you have a business book, by all means get it to the editor of the section. The savvy author reads the local paper to note names of writers and editors—most carry their emails within their tag lines—contact them when you like a story they've written. Send kudos. Keep your name out there. And, don't forget, most print papers have online versions.

Major Book Clubs

The Literary Market Place, LMP, has an extensive list of book clubs identifying areas of specialization. The primary ones fall under Direct Brands, Inc. Before contacting, make sure you have your phone pitch and letter pitch down—make sure it has a line about why your book is unique. If it is slated for major media attention, let them know. You can send galleys—many will take a book post printing. Follow-up, follow-up and follow-up again.

Direct Brands, Inc., Sharon Santera, Editorial Director, One Penn Plaza, 250 W. 34th St., 5th Floor, New York, NY 10119; Direct phone: 212-596-2297. Main phone: 212-901-0700. Web: *www.DirectBrands.com.* Email: *Sharon.Santera@DirectBrands.com.* Within Direct Brands, there are over 20 different clubs—from Book-of-the-Month to History to Children's. A few:

> Book-of-the-Month Club—includes most genres of fiction and nonfiction; *www.BOMCClub.com.*
>
> BOMC2—most genres of fiction and nonfiction; *www.BOMC2.com.*
>
> Doubleday Book Club—the latest fiction, nonfiction, romance and mystery; *www.DoubledayBookClub.com.*
>
> The Literary Guild—most genres of fiction and nonfiction; *www.LiteraryGuild.com.*
>
> Quality Paperback Book Club—soft cover editions of popular titles; *www.QPD.com.*

Serial & Excerpt Rights

Writer's Market is a good place to prospect for possible serial rights sales. Below are just a few:

Catholic Digest
Articles Editor, P.O. Box 6015, 1 Montauk Ave., Suite 200, New London, CT 06320, 800-321-0411, *www.CatholicDigest.com.*

Reader's Digest
Excerpt Editors, Reader's Digest Rd., Pleasantville, NY 10570, 914-238-1000, *www.RD.com*. Pitch article proposals online at *www.RD.com/articleProposalPage.do*.

USA Weekend
7950 Jones Branch Dr., McLean, VA 22107, *www.USAWeekend.com*.

Selected Wholesalers and Distributors

If your objective is to get your books into a bookstore or library, you need a wholesaler or a distributor. The *American Book Trade Directory* is available at your library (reference section) and an excellent source for contacts. Also check the *LMP*, then go to the website and verify if there are submissions info online.

Baker & Taylor
Publisher Contact Services, P.O. Box 6885, Bridgewater, NJ 08807-0885, *www.BTOL.com*. One of the two largest wholesalers (Ingram is the other).

Bookazine Company
75 Hook Rd., Bayonne, NJ 07002, 800-221-8112, *www.Bookazine.com*.

Books West
11111 E. 53rd Ave, Suite A, Denver, CO 80239, 800-378-4188, *www.BooksWest.net*. Serves Colorado and the West.

Coutts Library Services
P.O. Box 1000, 1823 Maryland Ave., Niagara Falls, NY 14302-1000; 800-686-2631, *www.CouttsInfo.com*.

DeVorss and Company
P.O. Box 1389, Camarillo, CA 93011-1389, 805-322-9010, *www.Devorss.com*. Metaphysical and spiritual books

Ingram Book Company
1 Ingram Blvd., La Vergne, TN 37086, 800-937-8200, *www.IngramBook.com*

Midpoint Trade Books
27 West 20th Street, Suite 1102, New York, NY 10011, 212-727-0190, *www.MidpointTrade.com*. Distributes for over 275 independent publishers.

Midwest Library Service
11443 St. Charles Rock Rd., Bridgeton, MO 63044-2789, 800-325-8833, *www.MidwestLS.com*.

New Leaf Distributing Company
401 Thornton Rd., Lithia Springs, GA 30057-1557, 770-948-7845, *www.Newleaf-Dist.com*. Metaphysical titles, New Age.

Pathway Book Service
P.O. Box 89, 4 White Brook Rd., Gilsum, NH 03448, 800-345-6665, *www.PathwayBook.com*. Fulfillment house and distributor for small presses.

Quality Books
1003 W. Pines Rd., Oregon, IL 61061-9680, 800-323-4241, *www.QualityBooks.com*. Library distributor for small presses.

Small Press Distribution
1341 Seventh St., Berkeley, CA 94710-1409, 800-869-7553, *www.SPDBooks.org*. Specializes in independently published literature.

Spring Arbor Distributors
One Ingram Blvd., La Vergne, TN 37086, 800-395-4340, *www.SpringArbor.com*. Main distributor of Christian books.

Unique Books
5010 Kemper Ave., St. Louis, MO 63139, 800-533-5446, *www.UniqueBooksInc.com*. Library distributor for small presses.

Video Plus
200 Swisher Rd., Lake Dallas, TX 75065, 800-752-2030, *www.VideoPlus.com*. Video distributor for personal development, health, home-based business, and personal finance.

Selected Bookstore Chains

Bookstores are changing—dominated by the chains—Barnes & Noble is king, there are several that you can pitch your book to. The store's parent website is where to go to get information on submission consideration and what to send. Always best to get a name; if impossible, otherwise send to fiction or nonfiction buyer. This is a PITCH. Have info on sales, marketing plans (they want to believe that you will drive buyers to their store), any book media kit. Assume that anything you send is theirs to keep. A few of the largest are:

American Wholesale Book Company (Books-A-Million)
Attn: New Acquisitions, 131 S. 25th St., Irondale, AL 35210, 205-956-4151. Makes recommendations to Walmart as well.

Barnes & Noble/Doubleday
Small Press Department, 122 5th Ave., 4th Floor, New York, NY 10011, 212-633-3300, *www.BarnesAndNoble.com.* Buys for all stores in chain.

Borders/Waldenbooks
New Vendor Acquisitions, 100 Phoenix Dr., Ann Arbor, MI 48108 734-477-1100, *www.Borders.com.* Details and guidelines on how to list your books on website.

Costco Wholesale
Attn: Book Buying Department, New Book Submissions, 999 Lake Dr., Issaquah, WA 98027, 425-313-8100, *www.Costco.com.*
Send book with sales info, press kit and name of distributor.

Follett Higher Education Group
1818 Swift Dr., Oak Brook, IL 60523, 800)-323-4506, 630-279-2330, *www.FHEG.Follett.com.* Submission info is found under "contact us."

Selected Book Review Sources

Authors want reviews, especially good ones. Below are key newspaper and magazine book reviewers. Select what's appropriate for your book.

Alternative Press Review
P.O. Box 6245, Arlington, VA 22206, 314-442-4352, *www.ALTPR.org*

The Bloomsbury Review
1553 Platte St., Suite 206, Denver, CO 80202-1167, 303-455-3123, *www.BloomsburyReview.com*

The Bookwatch/Midwest Book Reviews
278 Orchard Dr., Oregon, WI 53575-1129, 608-835-7937, *www.MidwestBookReview.com* (IBPA and SPAN member titles get preferential treatment.)

The Christian Science Monitor
210 Massachusetts Ave., Boston, MA 02115, 617-450-7929, *www.CSMonitor.com*

Gannett News Service
Gannett Company, Inc., 7950 Jones Branch Dr., McLean, VA 22107-1050, 703-854-6000, *www.Gannett.com*. Gannett is everywhere.

Newsday
235 Pinelawn Rd., Melville, NY 11747, 631-843-4659, *www.Newsday.com*

Parade
711 Third Ave., New York, NY 10017, *www.Parade.com*

Rainbo Electronic Reviews
5405 Cumberland Rd., Minneapolis, MN 55410, 610-408-4057, *www.RainboReviews.com*

The San Diego Union-Tribune
P.O. Box 120191, San Diego, CA 92112-0191, 800-533-8830, *www.SignonSanDiego.com*

San Francisco Chronicle
901 Mission St., San Francisco, CA 94103, 415-777-1111, *www.SFGate.com*

United Feature Syndicate, Inc.
200 Madison Ave., 4th Floor, New York, NY 10016, 212-293-8500, *www.UnitedFeatures.com*

United Press International
1133 19th St. N.W., Washington, DC 20036, 202-898-8000, *www.UPI.com*

Universal Press Syndicate
1130 Walnut St., Kansas City, MO 64106-2109, 816-581-7300, *www.AMUniversal.com/ups/submissions.htm*

USA Today
1000 Wilson Boulevard, Arlington, VA 22229. *www.USAToday.com*
See updated editors at USAToday website.

The Wall Street Journal
1211 Avenue of the Americas, New York, NY 10036, 212-416-2000, *http://online.WSJ.com*

Washington Post
1150 15th St., N.W., Washington, DC 20071, *www.WashingtonPost.com*

Selected Online Resources

There are so many online review resources—check websites for submission guidelines. Below are just a few:

Book Blogs Ning
http://BookBlogs.ning.com
Expose yourself! Offer your book for review on this social network site—thousands of members.

BookHitch.com
www.BookHitch.com
Free or paid listings.

BookLoons.com
www.BookLoons.com

Features a variety of books—romance, sci-fi, mystery, teens, children—just about anything. Updated weekly.

BookPage.com
www.BookPage.com
Includes a library of well-written book reviews in many genres, including a section on children's books, blogs and a newsletter.

FeatheredQuill.com
www.FeatheredQuill.com
Pay-for-review site that focuses on self-published and small press books.

The New Book Review
www.TheNewBookReview.blogspot.com
Composite of reviews from readers, authors and reviewers. The New Book Review was named to Online Universities' 101 Best Blogs for Readers.

Media Access

Author 101™ Million-Dollar Rolodex 2010
Rick Frishman rick@rickfrishman.com
www.RickFrishman.com
Will counsel you on all types of media and marketing. Rick works with several media companies and can help you. Tons of resources that's updated annually—Log on and get your copy.

Gebbie Media Directories
www.GebbieInc.com
Directories and online press releases.

Internet News Bureau
www.NewsBureau.com
Online news release service.

Media Finder
www.MediaFinder.com
Newsletters, magazines and catalogs

Planned TV Arts

www.PlannedTVArts.com

Offers Morning Drive Radio Tours, satellite tours, teleprint conferences and regular publicity services.

PR Leads

www.PRLeads.com

Hone in to your niche with Dan Janal who will personally assist you as you build your media database.

PR Newswire

www.PRNewswire.com

Sends news releases to targeted or all media nationally and internationally. Radio, newspaper, Internet and top national TV—over 4,000 contacts.

Promising Promotion/Jill Lublin

www.JillLublin.com

Public Relations Training Programs, Speaking and Consulting

Publicity Hound

www.PublicityHound.com

Joan Stewart serves up a variety of free tips, tricks and tools for free publicity.

The Publicity Vault (Alex Carroll's Radio Publicity Home Study Course)

www.PublicityVault.com

Created by Alex Carroll, the ultimate in learning how to book yourself onto the largest radio shows.

QuickSilver Database

www.BookPublishing.com

Over 17,000 media contacts created by the Jenkins Group.

RTIR - Radio TV Interview Report

www.RTIR.com Steve Harrison

Send a description of your book, what your expertise is and media pitch to more than 4,000 radio and TV producers. Bradley Communications and RTIRs in-house experts will help you design your ads and pitch.

The Spizman Agency
www.SpizmanAgency.com Willy Spizman
Full-service public relations and media placement firm specializing in book, expert and author promotion.

Talkers Directory of Talk Radio, Talkers Magazine
www.Talkers.com
Features the names, addresses, phone, fax, email, and web site info on hundreds of talk stations and individual hosts.

Books for Your Personal Publishing Shelf

Writing and Editing

The Chicago Manual of Style, Fifteenth Edition. University of Chicago Press: 2003. Standard style guide for publishers and editors. Fundamentals of Grammar, punctuation, etc.

The Complete Guide to Editing Your Fiction by Michael Seidman. Writer's Digest Books: 2002. Shows how to use "macro editing," style editing and market editing to create a polished, publishable piece.

The Copywriter's Handbook, Third Edition, by Robert W. Bly. Henry Holt: 2006. Write copy that sells.

The Elements of Style: The Original Edition by William Strunk Jr. Waking Lion Press: 2009. Updated and should be a once a year read for all writers.Fundamentals of writing.

ePublish: Self-Publish Fast and Profitably by Steve Weber. Weber Books: 2009. All about Kindle, iPhone, CreateSpace and Print on Demand.

From Book to Market by Joanna Penn. LuLu: 2009. All about selling your book via your website; includes the author's award-winning book marketing plan.

Grammar Girl's Quick and Dirty Tips for Better Writing (Quick & Dirty Tips) by Mignon Fogarty. Holt: 2008. Find your grammar groove with the Grammar Girl.

Grammatically Correct by Anne Stilman. Writer's Digest Books: 2004. A reference for punctuation, spelling, style usage, and grammar.

How to Write a Movie in 21 Days: The Inner Movie Method by Viki King. Quill: 2001. Learn the insider's technique on how to get the movie in your heart onto the page.

Save the Cat! The Last Book on Screenwriting That You'll Ever Need by Blake Snyder. Michael Wiese Productions. 2005. Practical, and fun, guide to writing mainstream spec scripts.

The Marshall Plan Workbook by Evan Marshall. Writer's Digest Books: 2001.Creative way to help write a novel, scene-by-scene.

On Writing: A Memoir of the Craft by Stephen King. Scribner: 2000. Excellent source to inspire writers—new and old—from ideas to writing to sales. King calls it his "curriculum vitae."

On Writing Well: 30th Anniversary Edition: The Classic Guide to Writing Nonfiction by William K. Zinsser. Harper Paperbacks: 2006. An outstanding book for every nonfiction writer.

Stet! Tricks of the Trade for Writers and Editors by Bruce O. Boston. Editorial Experts, Inc.: 1986. Handy editing tool for when the manuscript comes back from the editor.

Story: Substance, Structure, Style and the Principles of Screenwriting by Robert McKee. HarperCollins: 1997. For fiction and screenwriting, Story belongs on your bookshelf.

The Writer's Journey: 2nd Edition-Mythic Structure for Writers by Christopher Vogler. Michael Wise Productions: 1998. Dissects why great movies are structured the way they are by the author who has evaluated over 10,000 screenplays for major motion picture studios.

Publishing

The Complete Guide to Self-Publishing by Marilyn Ross and Sue Collier. Writer's Digest: 2010. Excellent resource, exceeding 500 pages on just about everything you need to know in today's publishing world—includes updates on social media.

Getting It Printed, Fourth Edition, by Mark Beach and Eric Kenley. HOW Books: 2004. Easily understood examples of how to work with printers and graphic arts services.

Methods of Book Design, Third Edition, by Hugh Williamson. Yale University Press: 2009. All about book cover design.

Recipe for a Cookbook: How to Write, Publish, and Promote Your Cookbook by Gloria Chadwick. Copper Canyon Books: 2008. Ways to create a readable cookbook along with strategies to promote it.

Self-Publishing Manual, 16th Edition by Dan Poynter. Para Publishing: 2007. Almost everything you need to know about publishing and didn't know to ask.

Self-Publishing Manual, Vol. 2 by Dan Poynter. Para Publishing: 2009. The sequel to almost everything you need to know about publishing with new technology and didn't know to ask.

Writing Creative Nonfiction: Fiction Techniques for Crafting Great Nonfiction by Theodore A. Rees Cheney. Story Press: 2001. Transition from boring to exciting. Techniques to make your words soar.

Writing Nonfiction: Turning Thoughts into Books, Fourth Edition, by Dan Poynter. Para Publishing: 2005. How to write, publish and promote nonfiction.

The Writer's Digest Flip Dictionary by Barbara Ann Kipfer. Writer's Digest Books: 2000. Excellent reference for terms and phrases. Fun book.

You Can Write a Novel Kit by James V. Smith, Jr. Writer's Digest Books: 2008. Perfect for first-time novelists in creating characters, scenes and plots.

Marketing & Media

1001 Ways to Market Your Books by John Kremer. Open Horizons: 2007. The bible of marketing, belongs on every author's bookshelf.

The Author's Guide to Building an Online Platform: Leveraging the Internet to Sell More Books by Stephanie Chandler. Quill Driver Books: 2008. Build an international platform right from your kitchen table.

Beyond the Bookstore by Brian Jud. Reed Publications: 2004. Ideal for any author seeking strategies for marketing books within the niche markets.

Blogging for Business: Everything You Need to Know and Why by Shel Holtz and Ted Demopoulos. Kaplan Business: 2006. How to tap into the power of blogging.

Burrelles Luce Media Directory. Print, broadcast and Web news sources. Provides online access to current media contacts. Online only—go to *www.BurrellesLuce.com*.

The Findability Formula by Heather Lutze. John Wiley & Sons: 2009. Sub title says it all: The Easy, Non-Technical Approach to Search Engine Marketing. Find Heather at *www.FindabilityFormula.com*.

Grassroots Marketing for Authors and Publishers by Shel Horowitz. Accurate Writing and More: 2009. Tips and strategies for maximizing marketing efforts at minimal costs.

Guerrilla Marketing for Writers: 100 No-Cost, Low-Cost Weapons for Selling Your Book by Jay Conrad Levinson, Rick Frishman, David Hancock and Michael Larsen. Morgan James: 2010. One hundred terrific ideas for selling your work and book.

Guerrilla Publicity: Hundreds of Sure-Fire Tactics to Get Maximum Sales for Minimum Dollars by Jay Conrad Levinson, Rick Frishman and Jill Lublin. Adams Media: 2002. Terrific and smart tips on getting publicity anywhere.

How to Get on Radio Talk Shows All Across America without Leaving Your Home or Office. Pacesetter Publications: 2006. Strategies for how to sell more books on the radio. Author creates an updated list of radio shows every January and is available through website, *www.JoeSabah.com.*

How to Make Real Money Selling Books (Without Worry About Returns) by Brian Jud. Square One Publishers: 2009. Sell books outside the normal bookstore methods.

T*he New Rules of Marketing and PR: How to Use News Releases, Blogs, Podcasting, Viral Marketing and Online Media to Reach Buyers Directly,* Revised Edition, by David Meerman Scott. John Wiley & Sons: 2009. Maximize Web-based communication.

Plug Your Book! Online Book Marketing for Authors by Steve Weber. Weber Books: 2007. Make your book stand out on the Internet.

Red Hot Internet Publicity: An Insider's Guide to Promoting Your Book on the Internet by Penny C. Sansevieri. Cosimo Books: 2009. Offers strategies and tips for online book promotion. Follow Penny on Twitter @BookGal.

Turn Eye Appeal into Buy Appeal by Karen Saunders. Macgraphics Services: 2006. Award-winning book that shows you how to create marketing pieces that become excellent and persuasive sales tools. Sign up for free monthly newsletters at *www.MacGraphics.net.*

Twitter Revolution: How Social Media and Mobile Marketing are Changing the Way We Do Business & Market Online by Warrren Whitlock and Deborah Micek. Xeno Press: 2008. Designed for anyone using Twitter.

Business Procedures

Book Design and Production by Pete Masterson. Aeonix Publishing Group: 2005. Explains the book production process and the principles of good cover and interior book design.

Contract Companion for Writers by Tonya M. Evans. Legal Write Publications: 2007. How to guide for standard writer and author contracts. Includes CD of all forms.

Copyright Companion for Writers by Tonya M. Evans. Legal Write Publications: 2007. Excellent resource to protect writers.

The Copyright Handbook: What Every Writer Needs to Know, Tenth Edition, by Stephen Fishman J.D. NOLO: 2008.

Kirsch's Handbook of Publishing Law by Jonathan Kirsch. Acrobat Books: 1994.Clear, comprehensive publishing law.

Literary Law Guide for Authors: Copyright, Trademark & Contract by Tonya M. Evans. Legal Write Publications: 2003. Straight-forward information on sticky questions on fair usage, trademarks and contracts.

The Profitable Publisher: Making the Right Decisions by Marion Gropen. Gropen & Associates: 2010. The nitty gritty techniques that solve problems all small publishers face—in ebook format. First book in a series.

Publishing for Profit: Successful Bottom-Line Management for Book Publishers, Second Edition, by Thomas Woll. Chicago Review Press: 2010. Publishing is a business. Learn how to set it up and run it effectively and efficiently.

References

Author 101: Bestselling Book Proposals: The Insider's Guide to Selling Your Work, Rick Frishman and Robyn Freedman Spizman with Mark Steisel. Adams Media: 2005. Take your book from manuscript to market.

Encyclopedia of Associations. Gale Research Company: 2009. Published annually, lists societies, associations and groups representing virtually any subject. Ideal to use to identify groups to market to for book reviews, sales and speaking opportunities.

Jeff Herman's Insider's Guide to Book Publishers, Editors and Literary Agents 2010 by Jeff Herman. Three Dogs Press: 2009. Updated annually, identifies players and contacts within publishing.

Literary Market Place (LMP). R.R. Bowker: 2010. A comprehensive list of prime contacts; published annually. A must-have for every self-publisher's library.

The Standard Periodical Directory. Oxbridge Communications, Inc.: 2009. Guide to U.S. and Canadian periodicals.

Ulrich's International Periodicals Directory. R.R. Bowker: 2009. Information on more than 300,000 periodicals.

Words That Sell, Revised and Expanded Edition: The Thesaurus to Help You Promote Your Products, Services, and Ideas by Richard Bayan. McGraw-Hill: 2006. Every author needs a thesaurus—this one will be of great assistance in marketing and creating copy.

Writer's Market, edited by Robert Lee Brewer. Writer's Digest Books: 2010. Annual volume that contains excellent marketing sources.

Books in Print, 2008–2009. R.R. Bowker: 2008. Annual listing of all in-print titles from thousands of publishers—bookstores carry the online version, using it to identify books, authors and publishers for ordering.

Merriam-Webster's Collegiate Dictionary, Eleventh Edition, Merriam-Webster: 2003. A comprehensive and excellent dictionary.

The Random House Webster's College Dictionary. Random House: 2000. A Comprehensive and excellent dictionary.

Small Press Record of Books in Print, 2008–2009, edited by Len Fulton. Dustbooks: 2008. Annually revised with lists by author, title, publisher and subject.

Roget's Thesaurus of Phrases by Barbara Ann Kipfer. Writer's Digest Books: 2000. Excellent tool using multiword entries and synonyms.

Wikipedia The best first research source to look for an overview of almost any subject, as long as you know that it's only a starting place for research. Caution: Wikipedia is not the definitive source.

Writer's Digest. Writer's Digest Books Magazine. Has market information, getting-published aids, and how-to articles.

Book and Author Award Programs

There are many awards given out to books and authors every year.

Why go for awards?

Because they will help you sell books. As five-time RITA award-winning author Jo Beverley noted, "Whenever you win, it makes it easier to sell your work."

Similarly Leslie Wagner, senior editor at Silhouette, uses the designation, 'RITA Award-winning author' on covers whenever she can because, "It's one other piece that makes the books stand out in a crowded marketplace."

Acupuncture Book of the Year Award, Acupuncture.com, Johanna Masse, Yo San Books, 13315 Washington Boulevard #200, Los Angeles CA 90066; 310-302-1207. Email: *JMasse@TaoStar.com*.

American Horticultural Society Awards, 7931 East Boulevard Drive, Alexandria VA 22308; 703-768; Fax: 703-768-8700. Each year AHS honors great gardening literature through the AHS Book Award Program, including children's and adult gardening books.

Arizona Book Awards, Arizona Book Publishing Association, Gwen Henson, Executive Director, 6340 S Rural Road #118-152, Tempe AZ 85283; 602-274-6264; Gwen: 480-777-9250; Email: *AZBookawards@gmail.com*. Awards for books written by an Arizona author, published by an Arizona publisher, or set in Arizona.

ASPCA Henry Bergh Children's Book Awards, ASPCA Education Department, 424 East 92nd Street, New York NY 10128; 212-876-7700. Deadline: October 31st, with awards presented at the American Library Association Convention during the next summer. Awarded to outstanding children's books that foster empathy, compassion, and respect for living beings.

Association for Library Service to Children Awards, 50 E Huron St., Chicago IL 60611; 800-545-2433. Email: *alsc@ala.org. Awards details: http://www.ALA.org/ala/alsc/awardsscholarships/ awardsscholarships.htm.* Awards for children's book authors and illustrators, including the Newbery Medal, Caldecott Medal, and more.

Audie Awards, Audio Publishers Association, 191 Clarksville Road, Princeton Junction NJ 08550; 609-799-6327; Fax: 609-799-7032. Email: *Info@AudioPub.org.* Annual awards prior to BookExpo America with many awards in various categories for spoken word audio.

The Irma Simonton Black and James H. Black Award, 610 West 112th Street, New York NY 10025; 212-875-4540. Email: *BookCom@BankStreet.edu.* Given to a picture book for children, grades 1 through 3, that is considered the best for text and illustration.

Books for a Better Life Awards, National Multiple Sclerosis Society, New York City Chapter; 212-463-7787. Offers awards for first book, inspirational memoir, motivational, psychology, relationships, spiritual, and wellness. Very New York publisher oriented in its selections.

Boston Globe / Horn Book Awards, Sarah Scriver, 56 Roland Street #200, Boston MA 02129; 617-628-0225. Email: *SScriver@HBook.com.* Categories: picture book, children's fiction and poetry, and children's nonfiction. Submissions: *http://www.HBook.com/bghb/submissions_bghb.asp.*

Rachel Carson Environment Book Award, Society of Environmental Journalists, P O Box 2492, Jenkintown PA 19046; 215-884-8174. Email: *SEJ@SEJ.org.* Annual award with a $10,000 prize.

CBHL Literature Award, Council on Botanical and Horticultural Libraries. Recognizes a general interest and technical book making a significant contribution to botany and horticulture. Online submission form.

The Children's Book Committee at Bank Street College, 610 West 112th Street, New York NY 10025; 212-875-4540. Email: *BookCom@bankstreet.edu.* The Josette Frank Award for children's fiction and the Flora Stieglitz Straus Award for children's nonfiction.

Christian Small Publisher Book of the Year, Christian Small Publishers Association, Sarah Bolme, P O Box 481022, Charlotte, NC 28269; 704-277-7194; Fax: 704-717-2928. Email: *CSPA@ChristianPublishers.net.* Honors fiction, nonfiction, and children's books produced by small publishers each year for outstanding contribution to Christian life.

Christopher Awards, Judith Trojan, Program Manager, The Christophers, 12 East 48th Street, 4th Floor, New York NY 10017; 212-759-4050; Fax: 212-838-5073. Email: *J.Trojan@Christophers.org.* Presented annually to writers, producers, directors, and illustrators in the publishing, film, broadcast TV, and cable industries for works that "affirm the highest values of the human spirit."

Business Book Awards, Kate Mytty; 414-274-6406. Email: *Kate@800ceoread.com.* Thirteen categories: sales, leadership, human resources, entrepreneurship/small business, finance/economics, advertising/marketing, globalization, fables, biographies/memoirs, personal development, innovation/creativity, industry, and new perspectives.

EVVY Awards—Colorado Independent Publishers Association—annual awards in a variety of categories. Deadline for submissions is in January. *www.CIPABooks.com.* Must be a member.

Firecracker Alternative Book Awards — Awards for gay/lesbian, alternative cultural books, etc. Given out at BEA every year. Horrible web site. Unless you allow Flash to work, you have no access to this web site. No alternatives to this alternative web site.

First Book Prize in Photography, Center for Documentary Studies, Duke University, 1317 W Pettigrew Street, Durham NC 27705; 919-660-3663.

ForeWord Magazine's Book of the Year Awards, ForeWord, 129½ E. Front Street, Traverse City MI 49684; 231-933-3699; Fax: 231-933-3899. *www.ForewordMagazine.com.* Forty plus categories of awards.

Benjamin Franklin Book Awards, Independent Book Publishers Association, 627 Aviation Way, Manhattan Beach CA 90266; 310-372-2732; Fax: 310-374-3342. Email: *Info@IBPA-online.org*. Annual awards prior to BookExpo America with more than 100 categories, all subjects and formats. One of the most prestigious of awards now being presented.

Garden Globe Awards, Garden Writers Association of America, 10210 Leatherleaf Court, Manassas VA 20111; 703-257-1032; Fax: 703-257-0213. Email: *Info@GWAA.org*. Web: *www.GWAA.org*. Since the early 1980s, the GWAA annual awards program has recognized outstanding writing, photography, graphic design and illustration for books, newspaper stories, magazine articles, and other works focused on gardening. In recent years awards have expanded to include on-air talent, production and direction for radio, television, video, Internet and other electronic media.

Georgia Author of the Year Awards, Georgia Writers Association, English Department #2701, Kennesaw State University, 1000 Chastain Road, Kennesaw GA 30144; 770-420-4736. Email: *RTWilson@Kennesaw.edu*. Awards for fiction, first novel, memoir, history, self-help, essay, inspirational, specialty books, poetry, short stories/anthologies, young adult, middle readers, and picture books. Nomination forms at *http://www.GeorgiaWriters.org/gayanom-43rd.pdf*.

Griffin Poetry Prize, The Griffin Trust for Excellence in Poetry, Toronto, Canada; 905-565-5993. International and Canadian poetry prizes ($40,000 each).

Eric Hoffer Book Award, Hopewell Publications, P O Box 11, Titusville NJ 08560; Fax: 609-818-1913. Email: *HofferAward@yahoo.com*. $40 entry fee. Awards in art, fiction, commercial fiction, young adult, culture, business, reference, home, health/self-help, and legacy (titles over two years old). Plus individual press awards to micro press, small press, academic press, and self-published.

Independent Publisher Book Awards (IPPY), Jim Barnes, Managing Editor, 400 W Front Street #4A, Traverse City MI 49684; 231-933-0445; 800-706-4636; Fax: 231-933-0448. Email: *JIMB@BookPublishing.com*. Annual awards just prior to BookExpo America every year. Online entry form at: *http://www.IndependentPublisher.com/ipland/IPAwards.php*.

International Automotive Media Awards, Walter Haessner, Executive Director; 520-749-2260; Fax: 520-792-8501. Email: *WRH@aztexcorp.com*.

Kiriyama Pacific Rim Book Prize, Kiriyama Pacific Rim Institute, Jeannine Cuevas, Prize Manager; 415-777-1628. Web: *www.PacificRimVoices.org*. Honors books that "encourage greater understanding among the peoples and nations of the Pacific Rim." Winners, who win $15,000, are announced in October.

Legacy Awards for Black Writers—The Hurston/Wright Foundation and Borders Books honor innovative black writers in three categories: literary fiction, nonfiction, and debut/first fiction.

Lukas Prize Project, 212-854-8653. Email: *Lukas@JRN.Columbia.edu*. The $10,000 J. Anthony Lukas Prize is given annually to a book of narrative non-fiction on a topic of American political or social concern. Also the $10,000 Mark Lynton History Prize is given to a work of narrative history on any subject. Finally, the $45,000 J. Anthony Lukas Work-in-Progress is given annually to aid the completion of a significant work of non-fiction. All three prizes are jointly administered by the Graduate School of Journalism at Columbia University and the Nieman Foundation for Journalism at Harvard University. Deadline: early December.

John T. Lupton New Voices In Literature Awards, Books for Life Foundation; 317-685-2500. A prize of $10,000 is awarded to winners in both the fiction and nonfiction categories.

Macavity Awards, Mystery Readers International. Announced annually at the World Mystery Convention. For information, contact Janet A. Rudolph, editor, Mystery Readers Journal; 510-845-3600; Email: *WhoDunIt@MurderOnTheMenu.com*.

Mom's Choice Awards, Bumble Bee Productions, 725 Watch Island Reach, Chesapeake VA 23320; 757-410-9409.
Email: *MomsChoiceAwards@bbpmail.com*. Recognizes authors, inventors, companies, parents, and others for their efforts in creating quality family-friendly media products and services. Awards in 50 categories.

Moonbeam Children's Awards, 1129 Woodmere, Suite B, Traverse City, MI 49686. 800.706.4636. *www.MoonbeamAwards.com*. Moonbeam Children's Book Awards are designed to bring increased recognition to exemplary children's books and their creators, and to support childhood literacy and life-long reading. Awards will be given in 36 categories covering the full range of subjects, styles and age groups that children's books are written and published in today.

National Book Awards, The National Book Foundation, 99 Madison Avenue #709, New York NY 10016; 212-685-0261; Fax: 212-213-6570. Email: *NationalBook@NationalBook.org*. $125 per entry. Entry information: *http://www.nationalbook.org/nbaentry.html*. Awards in fiction, nonfiction, poetry, and young people's literature.

According to the *Wall Street Journal*, the National Book Awards confer "significant sales to little-known works of fiction." 92% of the 30,799 copies of William Vollman's *Europe Central* were sold after the novel won the 2005 award. 96% of the 36,893 copies of Kevin Boyle's *Arc of Justice* were sold after the novel won the 2004 award. Lily Tuck's *The News from Paraguay* sold 60,000 copies after winning the award. Prior to the award, her book had sold 14,000 copies.

National Indie Excellence Awards, 269 S Beverly Drive #1065, Beverly Hills CA 90212; 805-884-9996; Fax: 805-884-9911.
Email: *Support@IndieExcellence.com*. Presents an opportunity for all independent publishers, small presses, self-publishers, and POD authors. Entry deadline: March 31st each year.

National Jewish Book Award, Jewish Book Council, 520 8th Avenue, 4th Floor, New York NY 10018; 212-201-2920; Fax: 212-532-4952.
Email: *JBC@JewishBooks.org*. Since 1950. Awarded to a Jewish-related book every year.

National Outdoor Book Awards (NOBA), Ron Watters, Iowa State University, Ames IA; 208-282-3912; Fax: 208-282-4600. Email: *Wattron@ISU.edu*. Awards for outdoors history/biography, outdoors literature, outdoor classic, design & artistic merit, children's books, nature/environment, nature guidebook, instructional, and outdoor adventure guidebook. Very open to small publishers.

Nautilus Book Awards, Marilyn McGuire & Associates, P O Box 400, Eastsound WA 98245; 360-376-2001. Email: *Marilyn@MarilynMcguire.com*. Awards for mind/body/spirit books and audios.

New Mexico Book Awards, Paul Rhetts & Barbe Awalt, NM Book Co-op, 925 Salamanca NW, Los Ranchos de Albuquerque, NM 87107; 505-344-9382. Email: *Info@NMBookCoop.com*. The books must have some connection to New Mexico or the Southwest, either via the subject, the author, or the publisher. Lots of categories, including children's, arts, biography, history, cookbooks, business, reference, religion, self-help, travel, poetry, and more. Plus five fiction categories and anthologies.

Parent's Choice Award: Honors the best material for children, including books, toys, music and storytelling, magazines, software, videogames, television and websites. Parents' Choice Foundation, Suite 303, 201 West Padonia Rd.,Timonium, MD 21093, 410-308-3858. *www.Parents-Choice.org*.

PNBA Book Awards, Thom Chambliss, Director, Pacific Northwest Booksellers Association, 214 East 12th Avenue, Eugene OR 97401-3245; 541-683-4363; Fax: 541-683-3910. *www.PNBA.org*. Email: *Info@PNBA.org*.

Purple Dragonfly Book Awards, Linda Radke, Five Star Publications; 480-940-8182. Email: *Info@FiveStarPublications.com*. Honors authors of children's books for kids ages 4 to 10.

RITA Awards, Romance Writers Association. *www.RWANational.org*. This national association of romance writers offers awards in a variety of romance novel categories.

Sami Rohr Prize for Jewish Literature, Jewish Book Council, 520 8th Avenue, 4th Floor, New York NY 10018; 212-201-2920; Fax: 212-532-4952. *www.JewishBooks.org*. Email: *JBC@JewishBooks.org*. Submissions are not accepted. An advisory panel searches for eligible works.

The annual award recognizes the unique role of contemporary writers in the transmission and examination of Jewish values, and is intended to encourage and promote outstanding writing of Jewish interest. Each year, the prize of $100,000 will aim to reward an emerging writer whose work has demonstrated a fresh vision and evidence of future potential. Recipients must have written a book of exceptional literary merit that stimulates an interest in themes of Jewish concern. Fiction and non-fiction books are considered in alternate years.

Self-Published Book Awards, Writer's Digest, 1507 Dana Avenue, Cincinnati OH 45207. *www.WritersDigest.com*. Annual awards with a mid-December deadline for applications.

Teen Development Awards, Justin Sachs, Awards Director. *http://VanPetten.TeenDevelopmentAwards.com/*

TIL Awards, Southwest Texas State University, San Marcos TX 78666; 512-245-2428; Fax: 512-245-7462. *www.TexasInstituteOfLetters.org*. Annual awards for short pieces, books, and book design. Open to Texas residents.

Dylan Thomas Prize, Tim Prosser, CEO; 44-1792-474051 or 44-7968-854435. *www.TheDylanThomasPrize.com*. They accept nominations for this £60,000 prize until April 30th of each year. The prize is awarded to the best book in English published by an author under 30.

The Prize aims to encourage, promote and reward exciting new writing in the English speaking world in commemoration of the life and work of Dylan Thomas. Entrants should be the author of a published book (in English), under the age of 30, writing within one of the following categories: poetry, novel, collection of short stories by one author, play that has been professionally performed, a broadcast radio play, a professionally produced screenplay that has resulted in a feature-length film. Authors need to be nominated by their publishers or producers (in the case of performance art).

USA Book News Awards JPX Media, USA Book News, PO Box 69408, Los Angeles, CA 90069, 800-733-6511, *www.USABookNews.com*. Over 70 categories that are specifically designed to garner media coverage for the winners and finalists throughout the following year. Submission deadline is July 31st with winners and finalists announced in October.

Washington Institute Book Prize, The Washington Institute for Near East Policy. *www.WashingtonInstitute.org*. Gold ($30,000), Silver ($15,000), and Bronze ($5,000) prizes for nonfiction books on the Middle East.

Canadian Contacts:

Association of Canadian Publishers (ACP)
www.Publishers.ca
Canadian trade organization representing Canadian owned book publishers.

Author's Choice Publishing Group
www.AuthorsChoice.ca
Publishes and distributes independent books.

The Book Trade in Canada
The annual *Book Trade in Canada* lists more than 800 publishers and 2,500 bookstores, editors, writers, printers, designers along with detailed information about book industry events—similar to the *LMP (Literary Market Place)* in U.S.

Canadian Authors Association (CAA)

www.CanAuthors.org
CAA publishes *The Canadian Author and Bookman* (quarterly writers'
magazine) and *The Canadian Writer's Guide*, a directory of writers'
markets.

Canadian Booksellers Association (CBA)

www.CBABook.org
Supports booksellers through education and services—smaller version of
BookExpo.

Doing Business in Canada

http://InvestInCanada.gc.ca
If you plan on selling in Canada, this online guide covers the Canadian
Goods and Services Tax or Harmonized Sales Tax(GST/HST). Website
has multiple language options. To download Canada Customs and
Revenue Agency's GST/HST forms, go to *www.CCRA-ADRC.gc.ca*.

Media Names and Numbers

www.Sources.com/mnnsubs.htm
Directory of Canadian print and broadcast media containing thousands
of contacts. If you are doing media in Canada, this one is for you.

Quill & Quire

P.O. Box 819, Markham, Ontario L3P 8A2, (800) 757-6177,
www.QuillAndQuire.com. Canadian monthly book trade magazine
comparable to *Publishers Weekly*. *Quill & Quire* also publishes the
Canadian Publishers Directory and *The Book Trade in Canada*.

Foreign Rights

Below is a partial list of several agencies that represent foreign rights.
Some of the addresses will take you directly to the contact list; for others,
you will need to click on a tab or put "foreign agents" in their search
window.

www.SwayzeAgency.com	Canada
www.OBrien.ie	Ireland

www.Escritores.org/recursos/agentes	Spanish
www.Esslinger-verlag.de/foreign/agenes.php	German
www.McClelland.com/rights	Multiple countries
www.RandomHouse.ca/rights	Multiple countries
www.ScribePub.com.au/rights	Multiple countries
www.TLA1.com	Canada, UK, Europe
www.Temple.edu/tempess/foreign_rights.hml	Multiple countries
www.NewMarketPress.com/foreignrights.asp	Multiple countries
www.Loewe-Verlag.de/rights/agencies.html	Multiple countries
www.SpectrumLiteracyAgency.com/foreign.htm	Multiple countries
www.Bob-Erdmann.com/foreign-rights.html	Multiple countries

For an updateded resource list you can go anytime to

http://:www.rickfrishman.com

and get our Million Dollar Rolodex

because information and contacts change often

Sneak Preview: Next in the *Show Me About* series ...

SHOW ME ABOUT BOOK PUBLICITY & SOCIAL MEDIA

Lights, Camera, Action, Online ... Are You Ready?

Judith Briles

Rick Frishman

John Kremer

WAHOO ...YOU ARE THE STAR!

Lights... Breathe deeply. Wiggle your hands and your feet.

Camera ... Do you direct all your comments to the host interviewing you, or do you speak towards the camera?—ask.

Action ...Your mic and/or camera is live ... smile ...

Wahoo ...You are on the air!

Experiences with the media can be exhilarating and fabulous. Or, they can be dismal and downright awful. How do you create the best media event possible and avoid the disasters that many authors encounter?

The answer is threefold:

- *Know your market.* If your book is a business leadership book, you want to be featured on shows that feature business leaders; are about management or careers; and have financial segments.

- *Know who carries programs that interview guests.* Start with Googling or Binging key words from your book or title; add in TV interviews, a selected city.

  Major cities usually publish *Business Journals*, i.e., *Denver Business Journal, Atlanta Business Journal, Minneapolis/St. Paul Business Journal.* These publications create an annual Book of Lists— within them are the top 25 media outlets for radio, TV and print. Names, addresses, phone numbers, websites.

- *Know which services to use to assist in getting the word out about you and your book.* Strategic ads can be placed. You pay for the services;

there are, of course, no guarantees. Here are a few that we've had success with over the years.

Steve Harrison created RTIR, Radio and TV Interview Reports, years ago (www.RTIR.com). RTIR is distributed twice a month to any producer that requests it. Loaded with ads that are pitch friendly for radio and TV, his team assists you in the creation— full page, half page, quarter page—it's your choice (of course you pay for it—the producers get it free). It's a way to get the word out quickly and one that producers hold on to for future guest ideas. He's also created Reporter Connection (*www.FreePublicity. com* or *www.ReporterConnection.com*) that sends out requests from media professionals looking for experts—you've got to wade through them.

Or, you can tap into Dan Janal's PR Leads (www.PRLeads.com). Janal has helped thousands of authors and small businesses get publicity to grow them, ID them as the expert in their topic field and promo their books. For a monthly (or annual) fee, you'll get an unlimited number of leads on a daily basis in your major areas of expertise. Not only do you identify your area, but he personally interviews you to make sure that you cover all your bases, tapping into areas that you hadn't thought of. A customized profile is created and then leads start rolling in, leads that should be relevant and therefore not waste your time in reading, much less pursuing.

PRWeb (www.PRWeb.com) is also a good landing spot for a media release that you've created that can be sent out in a mass broadcast to media outlets. You use its templates and create a media release that goes out to more than 30,000 opt-in journalists and bloggers (as well as Google and Yahoo!) where journalists look for story ideas and experts. Costs are minimal, starting at $80—If you are seeking viral coverage, this is a good place to start getting the word out.

HARO, known as Help a Reporter Out (www.HelpAReporterOut. com) hit the Internet and email boxes in 2008. Peter Shankman was a visionary in bringing sources and journalists together ...

for free. Creating the giant Rolodex in the virtual sky, journalists from anywhere in the world can toss out a query and the request goes to all the Sources. The responses come back from people they would have had to drill down to find, if they could. Authors, experts, anyone who has an interest in being featured in radio, TV and print (we are subscribers as Sources). This is a good resource.

According to radio publicity guru, Alex Carroll (www. RadioPublicity.com), radio programs throughout the United States need a collective 10,000 plus guests each day. Why not you? His learning curve started with his own experience. He self-published a book about how to beat traffic tickets and has generated book sales of over 100,000. He did it by pitching his book to radio shows. Carroll has determined that if he was a paid advertiser, he would have written checks for in excess of $4,500,000 to the station. Instead, he's received over $ 1,500,000 and been featured on 1200 (and counting) radio interviews. Carroll shows authors how to do what he did, and does.

- *Think local and regional.* Where do you live? Judith lives in Colorado; Rick in New York and John in New Mexico. Each state has major cities; Rick wins with the most. Each has the old fashion media: TV, radio and print.

For TV, major cities have major network affiliates: ABC, NBC, CBS, CNN and Fox. Some do extensive local morning, noon and evening news and community related programs. CNN isn't local, but usually has a coop arrangement with one of the affiliates (ABC, CBS or NBC) to use their studios/newsroom to interview a guest. Make a call—who is the primary "booker" for programming. Who is the news director?

For radio, it is common for multiple stations to be owned by the same media outlet. In Denver, Colorado, Clear Channel owns several radio stations—seven of them were moved to one main physical facility where a variety of shows are produced and aired throughout the day and night. Some shows are similar with different host personalities; some are as different as hot and cold.

For the author, this is comparable to mall shopping. You could physically be in the building and be interviewed on one show and 45 minutes later, another one. Different studio; different host; and usually, a different listening audience.

Or, you could be doing phoners—remote interviews where you either call in or the producer calls you. The bigger the show, the more likely there will be a separate producer versus having the host fill both roles.

The Media Is There

Yes, they can call you on their own with no contact initiated by you to start the ball rolling. But that's a remote possibility. To turn possibilities into probabilities, you initiate it. For radio and TV, all there for you to pick up the phone and ask …

- Do you have shows that have experts or authors as guests?
- Which ones are they?
- Who is the producer?
- Is there a preferred or best time to call?
- Could you give me their emails or direct phone line?

This is drill down time. Create a spread sheet so you can keep track of who to call and when you do. Make sure you add notes with date and time—could be as simple as:

6/12, 10:15a, lm re bk, new stats lying $

Translation: June 12th, 10:15 AM, left message about my book and what the new survey/poll I have with declining productivity results— what it means financially when management (or employees) lie in the workplace.

When you follow-up, you quickly review to have an inkling of what you left a message about a few days ago. You may repeat; add a variation/ twist; or you could leave different examples.

If your book is all about business and you somehow get yourself on a morning "zoo" type of program, it's most likely not the right fit. Whose fault is that? … the mirror will tell you.

Before you pick up that phone, you've got to put some energy and planning into creating the perfect pitch. When you get a producer on the phone, the odds are that if you blow it, you won't get another shot at it.

1. Keep it short … as in very brief … and clear. The number of emails and phone calls generated on a daily basis are overwhelming. If in writing—a great header, brief paragraph, maybe a couple of bullet points may just be the perfect pitch for a producer in a hurry who desperately needs a tantalizing four minute segment. Speak slooooooowly (especially when giving your call back number) and clearly. There is absolutely nothing more frustrating to a listener (meaning producer or reporter) if all he hears is incoherent mumble jumble on the other end—guaranteed, the message is trashed.

2. Create a strong hook.

3. Make sure you are clear on why you, and your book, are unique. Why should that producer care about what you have to say?

Use Your Website as a Pitcher, Too!

We are in the electronic age. That means you need to be able to communicate quickly and clearly; to be able to respond in a nanosecond when you are on the publicity trail; and have excellent material designed to cut to the chase—giving the media info on you and your book.

That means you need a website—a fresh and friendly one. Create a tab section that is all about your book. Include:

media releases	sample interview questions	photos
videos of shows	audios of shows	book trailer
list of appearances	articles featured in	book cover
kudos from interviews	Links to other sites	Blog

Websites are a critical part of your book persona. It's part of your branding—colors, graphics and personality. Mistakes that many authors make is to allow them to be stagnate—you need to add new material on an ongoing basis.

When you do get a live producer, ask if he is on the Internet (of course he is). Ask him to go to it so you can show him _____ (something fantastic/unique). He's there; the door is open; re-pitch your angle with a twist to it. Ask if your topic or angle is of interest. Ask if he would like material, including a book. Ask if he is interested in scheduling an interview. Ask when would be the best time to reconnect.

No matter what, send him a postcard, with the cover of your book, your contact info (including website) and a brief note thanking him for his time … even if he says, "No thank you."

That post card may just sit on his desk for a bit, reminding him of you, your book … and he has all your contact info—you never know.

ABOUT THE AUTHORS

Judith Briles, Rick Frishman and John Kremer speak throughout the United States and internationally. Each hosts websites, newsletters, blogs, and teleconferences that represent their respective areas of publishing expertise. Each has the platform to support the buzz factor for the **Show Me About Books** series.

Combined, they've published over 36 books and dozens of CDs, CD/ROMs, and DVDs. Foreign translations exceed 16 countries on their work.

Judith Briles

As the co-founder of Mile High Press, Ltd., a small press that has published nine titles (*www.MileHighPress.com*), founder of companies and organizations including: The Briles Group, Inc., a Colorado-based research, training and consulting firm (*www.Briles.com*); The Book Shepherd (*www.TheBookShepherd.com*), a company that works with authors to create, strategize, develop and publish their books; Author U (*www.AuthorU.org*), an association dedicated to the serious author who wants to create quality books and achieve financial success; and partner with the WebinarMentor.com, a company dedicated to the design and delivery of webinars.

She routinely consults with clients who are in the beginning stages of their books to implement an over-all plan to achieve book success. Judith Briles is known as The Book Shepherd. She knows publishing through the wearing of multiple hats: award-winning publisher (multiple first place awards for business, how to and publishing: technology printing, lay-out and cover design) and author (*Chicago Tribune's* Business Book of the Year, Colorado Book of the Year). The books of her clients routinely win awards in multiple publishing and author contests.

In 2007, she launched Judith's Publishing Salons, one-day intensives for authors and publishers in the areas of Newbies, Intermediate/Advanced, PR/Media, Speaking, Story Telling. PowerPoint Presentations and Webinars. She is internationally acclaimed as a speaker and recognized as an expert in solutions to workplace issues.

Judith is an award-winning author of 26+ books, including: *Stabotage!*™ *How to Deal with Pit Bulls, Skunks, Snakes, Scorpions & Slugs in the Health Care Workplace, Zapping Conflict in the Health Care Workplace, The Confidence Factor: Cosmic Gooses Lay Golden Eggs, Stop Stabbing Yourself in the Back, Woman to Woman: From Sabotage to Support, Woman to Woman 2000: Becoming Sabotage Savvy in the New Millennium, Money Smarts for Turbulent Times, Smart Money Moves for Kids and 10 Smart Money Moves for Women.* Her first book, *The Woman's Guide to Financial Savvy* was published in 1981 by St. Martin's Press. To date, her books have been translated in 16 foreign countries.

Her work has been featured in the *Wall Street Journal, Newsweek, Time, People, USA Today, Self, The New York Times* and *People* magazine. She has been a frequent guest on national television and radio and has appeared on over 1000 programs, including *CNN, Oprah* and *Good Morning America.* Judith writes regularly for a variety of publications.

She is a former President of The Colorado Author's League, the Colorado Independent Publishers Association (CIPA) and was honored with its Life Time Achievement Award. She is a past director of the National Speaker's Association; Gilda's Club-Denver; The WISH List; the Women's Bank and the Colorado Women's Leadership Coalition.

Colorado Biz magazine has named one of her companies as a Top 100 in Colorado. She was named the Woman of Distinction by the Girl Scouts of America.

Judith is married to John Maling and lives in Aurora, Colorado.

Rick Frishman

Is the founder of Planned Television Arts, has been one of the leading book publicists in America for over 33 years. Working with many of the top book editors, literary agents and publishers in America, including Simon and Schuster, Random House, Wiley, Harper Collins, Pocket Books, Penguin Putnam, and Hyperion Books, he has worked with best-selling authors including Mitch Albom, Bill Moyers, Stephen King, Caroline Kennedy, Howard Stern, President Jimmy Carter, Mark Victor Hansen, Nelson DeMille, John Grisham, Hugh Downs, Henry Kissinger, Jack Canfield, Alan Deshowitz, Arnold Palmer and Harvey Mackay.

Rick is the publisher at Morgan James Publishing in New York. In 2010, "MJ" published over 100 books. Morgan James only publishes non-fiction books and looks for authors with a platform who believe in giving back. Morgan James gives a portion of every book sold to Habitat for Humanity (www.MorganJamesPublishing.com).

Rick has also appeared on hundreds of radio shows and more than a dozen TV shows nationwide including *OPRAH* and *Bloomberg TV*. He has also been featured in the *New York Times, Wall Street Journal, Associated Press, Selling Power Magazine, New York Post* and scores of publications.

He is the co-author of 11 books, including national best-sellers *Guerrilla Publicity, Guerrilla Marketing for Writers-2nd Edition, Networking Magic* and *Where's Your WOW.*

He is the co-host (with attorney Richard Solomon) of the radio show *Taking Care of Business,* which airs every Thursday from 2:00-3:00 pm on *WCWP-Radio* in Long Island, New York (*www.TCBRadio.com*). Rick has a B.F.A. in acting and directing and a B.S. from Ithaca College School of Communications and he is a sought after lecturer on publishing and public relations and a member of PRSA and the National Speakers Association.

Rick and his wife Robbi live in Long Island with their three children, Adam, Rachel and Stephanie and two Havanese puppies, Cody and Cooper.

Go to *www.RickFrishman.com* for more information and to get Rick's "Million Dollar Rolodex." Also visit Rick at www.author101university.com.

John Kremer

As *the* acknowledged expert on book publishing and marketing, John Kremer is the owner of Open Horizons, his own publishing company based in Taos, New Mexico. He's been the editor of the *Book Marketing Update* newsletter for more than 20 years as well as editor of the *Kremer 100 PR* newsletter (*www.BookMarketing.com* and *www.JohnKremer.com*).

John is also the author of a number of books on publishing and marketing, including *1001 Ways to Market Your Books: For Authors and Publishers* (6th Edition), *The Complete Direct Marketing Sourcebook, High Impact Marketing on a Low Impact Budget* and *Celebrate Today.*

He has also designed the *Do-It-Yourself Book Publicity Kit*, the *Book Publishing Reports* on CD-Rom, and databases of the *Top 700 Booksellers, Specialty Booksellers, Catalogs That Feature Books, Public Libraries*, and *Seminar Centers.*

John consults in the areas of book marketing, book sales, book promotion, publicity, direct marketing, pricing, book titles, book covers, book marketing plans, book proposals, rights sales, and general planning for book publishers of all sizes as well as for individual authors. While most of John's consulting is done over the phone, he also provides on-site consulting services.

Among other services, he provided the strategy that took Deepak Chopra from a vanity press author to being on the *New York Times* bestseller list eight times. Jack Canfield and Mark Victor Hansen, authors of *Chicken Soup for the Soul*, credit John's book, *1001 Ways to Market Your Books*, as the guiding light for their rise to bestseller status.

As a consultant, his clients include a self-published author who has sold over two million books, a new age publisher with 60 titles, and a general publisher with a rapidly growing list of 1,500 titles.

John's consulting clients have gotten stories in the *Wall Street Journal, New York Times, Newsweek, Playboy, Scientific American, Chicago Tribune,*

Los Angeles Reader, as well as being featured on *Oprah, Today Show, Fresh Air, All Things Considered*, and many other local and national broadcast shows.

In addition, he was the original developer of the *Directory of Book Printers, Book Publishing Resource Guide, PR Profit Center* database, *Book Marketing No-Frills* database, and four special reports on publicity and specialty marketing.

He has spoken at book publishing and marketing seminars in New York, Los Angeles, San Francisco, San Diego, Chicago, Orlando, Miami, Denver, Boulder, Tucson, Portland, Seattle, Bellevue, San Antonio, Houston, Austin, Toronto, Kansas City, Milwaukee, Madison, Minneapolis, New Orleans, Phoenix, Kennebunkport, Saint Louis, Atlanta, Fresno, Indianapolis, Nashville, Saint Petersburg, West Palm Beach, Melbourne, Alexandria, Cincinnati, Buffalo, Sacramento, Ann Arbor, Grand Rapids, Des Moines, Cleveland, Omaha, Calgary, London, Las Vegas, Washington DC, and many other cities. His speeches have ranged from half-hour talks on book marketing to two-hour sessions on getting national publicity to three-day seminars on how to open new markets for your books.

John lives in Taos, New Mexico with his wife Gail and two dogs, Lisa and Elsie.

WE SPEAK …
WOULD YOU LIKE TO LISTEN?

Judith, John and Rick would be delighted to participate in your publishing conference or to speak to your group. If you want a highly interactive, informative and fun presentation or workshop, call them. To contact them about availability, call or email:

Judith Briles
Judith@TheBookShepherd.com
www.TheBookShepherd.com
www.AuthorU.org
www.Briles.com
303-627-9179 • 303-885-2207 Cell

Rick Frishman
Rick@RickFrishman.com
www.RickFrishman.com
516-308-1524

John Kremer
JohnKremer@BookMarket.com
www.JohnKremerSpeaker.com
www.BookMarket.com
575-751-3398

INDEX

A

Artists 24, 48, 50-1, 155
Author 101 4, 108, 172, 179
Amazon 12, 17, 28, 35,41, 89-90, 108, 112-3, 132, 143
Author U 4, 155

B

Back Matter 82, 87-8
Barcode 49, 87, 92
BISAC 92
Blogging 19, 58, 64, 70, 106-9, 117, 119, 121-2, 131-3, 139, 141, 150
Book Clubs 115, 144, 165-6
Book Coach 28, 29, 48, 53, 63-4, 75, 159
Book Consultant 53-4, 63, 65
Book Reviews 11, 165, 169
Book Shepherd 29, 39, 53, 55, 53-73, 131, 157-8, 160, 199
Book Signings xvii, 107, 114-5, 149
Books-In-Print 91, 110, 139, 156
Bookstores 16, 21, 34-5, 40-1, 53, 58-9, 67, 89-90, 92, 98, 107, 112, 188, 128, 141, 156,168, 180, 189

Branding 12, 72, 74, 107, 109, 139, 146-7, 198
Break-even 43-4

C

Covers 49-51, 62, 75, 89, 95-101
  Spines 49, 89, 97, 99
  Back 95-7
Cartoonists 48, 50-1, 72, 93
Copyright 21, 53, 82, 87-8, 90-3, 156-7, 178
Costs 21, 26, 35, 38-9, 42-4, 49, 58-9, 67, 81, 90, 123, 126, 139, 142, 177, 194
Cover Designs 25, 35-6, 48-9, 51, 61-5, 72, 74, 92, 96, 100, 103, 159, 175, 199
Credit Cards 38, 42, 109, 112, 120, 132, 143

D

Distributors 21, 37-8, 40-2, 58-9, 72, 91, 112,139, 167-9
Distribution 16, 59, 62, 158-160, 168

E

eBooks 16,27-8, 56, 71, 109,
    120, 126, 134, 145, 158,
    162, 168
Editors 3, 16, 18-9, 21, 26, 30,
    36, 48-9, 60-2, 77-85, 117,
    130, 138, 145, 154,159
    Copy-editing 83, 84, 145
    Line 83-4
    Developmental 79, 130
    Grammar 78
    Proofreading 79, 84
eMail Signature 111
Endorsements 19, 87-9, 97-9,
    103-6, 146

F

Facebook 67, 73, 107, 120-2,
    131, 145, 149
Failure 30
Financials 3, 24, 30, 33, 37, 45,
    55, 66, 110, 128, 193
Foreign rights 39, 123-8, 190
Front Matter 87-8
Fulfillment 6, 42-3, 59, 131, 159

G

Graphics 17, 48, 51-2, 80, 96,
    198
Graphic Designers 49

H

Hardback 6, 26, 33, 39-42, 87,
    93, 131
Hobbyist 3, 23, 37, 67

I

Illustrators 50-1, 72
Independent Books 16, 20
Independent Book Stores 108,
    147
Interior Designer 18-9, 21, 24,
    30, 36, 38, 48, 51-3, 65, 71,
    87, 94, 104, 145, 158, 161
iPad 17, 28, 56
ISBN 21, 26, 36-7, 43, 53, 87,
    90-2, 98, 103-4, 111, 125,
    131, 156

L

Library of Congress 21, 87, 91,
    103, 131, 156
LinkedIn 121, 131, 149
Literary Agents 61-2, 179
Lyrics 82, 93

M

Merchant Accounts 109
Mistakes 12-4,27, 48, 66, 70, 79,
    80, 104, 115, 139, 141, 150,
    198

N

Niche Publishing 5-6, 31, 65-6,
    89,110, 122, 136, 176

P

Pitching 16, 19,40, 59-61, 96-7,
    106-7, 112, 114-6, 118,
    121,144,148, 165, 194-5,
    197-8

Pitch Formula   107
Plan   6, 10, 24, 29-30, 38, 41-
    2, 51, 55, 57, 59, 60, 66-8,
    71-3, 75, 82, 98, 103, 119,
    129, 134, 137, 147-8
Platform   12, 19, 21, 38, 42, 58,
    60, 68, 73, 89, 106, 109,
    117-21, 131, 142
POD   3, 20, 25-7,36-7, 39,49,
    67, 69, 74, 103, 131, 144,
    161
Podcasting   107, 177
Pre-selling   106,120-1,139, 142
Pricing   6, 27, 41-45, 54-6, 57,
    87, 89-90, 98, 106, 111-2,
    120, 130, 142-3, 146
Printers   3, 10, 24,26, 30, 35-6,
    48, 51, 54-6, 65, 72, 79, 84,
    100, 103, 105, 131, 146-7,
    161-3
Printing   5-6,24, 26, 35-44, 54-6,
    60, 62, 67, 71, 74, 90, 103-
    5, 113,126, 129, 139, 143,
    146
    Digital   37-9, 54-6, 83, 105,
        146
    Offset   26,38-9,54-6,103, 105
Promo/PR   4, 15, 20, 65, 74,
    105-6, 108, 111, 113, 121,
    144
Publicity   30, 30, 70, 106, 108,
    111, 113, 125, 133, 148-9,
    191-8
Publishing Siren   9-10, 30, 151
Positioning   12-16, 31, 120, 125

Q
Quiz—
    Show Me About Book
        Publishing   1

R
Royalties   12-22, 34, 38-42, 61,
    124, 126

S
Scams   28, 60, 153
Social Media   43, 67, 107, 117-8,
    121-2, 131, 13, 149
    Blogging   19, 58, 64, 70,
        106-9, 117, 119, 121-2,
        131-3, 139, 141, 150
    Facebook   67, 73, 107, 120-2,
        131, 145, 149
    LinkedIn   121, 131, 149
    Twitter   107,119-22, 132-
        34, 139, 145, 149-50
Speaking   29, 41, 51, 66-7, 75,
    103, 108-9, 112-16,, 122-
    23, 131-32, 142-44

T
Ten Million EyeBalls   4, 228
Timelines   66, 103-118
Twitter   107,119-22, 132-34,
    139, 145, 149-50
Types of Publishing
    eBooks   27, 101, 117
    ePublishers   27-8
    Independent   24

Packagers   20, 25-6, 60, 70
Pay-to-Publish   15, 25, 60
POD   2, 37, 144
Self-Published   4, 15, 22-4,
        26, 36, 47, 54, 67, 74,
        77, 81, 90, 95, 144-45
Subsidy   20, 25
Traditional   2-4, 6, 12, 15-24,
        28-9, 32, 35, 38-42, 55,
        60, 63, 72, 75, 77, 90,
        101, 124, 131, 136, 145,
        148
Vanity Press   15-6, 26, 36-7

U

Unstuck (Getting)   129-34
URL   57, 107-08, 139

W

Websites   12, 37-8, 42-4, 48, 56-
        8, 71, 74, 84, 90, 106, 108,
        111, 113, 115-17, 120-22,
        125, 127, 137, 139-40, 142,
        144, 147, 158
Wholesalers   6, 21, 37-8, 40-4,
        58-9, 112, 139, 167
Why Publish   9, 18-20, 37-43

Y

Yin-Yang   12-3

BUY A SHARE OF THE FUTURE IN YOUR COMMUNITY

These certificates make great holiday, graduation and birthday gifts that can be personalized with the recipient's name. The cost of one S.H.A.R.E. or one square foot is $54.17. The personalized certificate is suitable for framing and will state the number of shares purchased and the amount of each share, as well as the recipient's name. The home that you participate in "building" will last for many years and will continue to grow in value.

Here is a sample SHARE certificate:

HABITAT FOR HUMANITY

THIS CERTIFIES THAT
YOUR NAME HERE
HAS INVESTED IN A HOME FOR A DESERVING FAMILY

1985-2005
TWENTY YEARS OF BUILDING FUTURES IN OUR COMMUNITY ONE HOME AT A TIME

1200 SQUARE FOOT HOUSE @ $65,000 = $54.17 PER SQUARE FOOT
This certificate represents a tax deductible donation. It has no cash value.

YES, I WOULD LIKE TO HELP!

I support the work that Habitat for Humanity does and I want to be part of the excitement! As a donor, I will receive periodic updates on your construction activities but, more importantly, I know my gift will help a family in our community realize the dream of homeownership. **I would like to SHARE in your efforts against substandard housing in my community!** *(Please print below)*

PLEASE SEND ME _____ SHARES at $54.17 EACH = $ $_____

In Honor Of: _____

Occasion: (Circle One)   HOLIDAY   BIRTHDAY   ANNIVERSARY

      OTHER: _____

Address of Recipient: _____

Gift From: _____ *Donor Address:* _____

Donor Email: _____

I AM ENCLOSING A CHECK FOR $ $_____ PAYABLE TO HABITAT FOR HUMANITY <u>OR</u> PLEASE CHARGE MY VISA OR MASTERCARD *(CIRCLE ONE)*

Card Number _____ Expiration Date: _____

Name as it appears on Credit Card _____ Charge Amount $ _____

Signature _____

Billing Address _____

Telephone # Day _____ Eve _____

PLEASE NOTE: Your contribution is tax-deductible to the fullest extent allowed by law.

Habitat for Humanity • P.O. Box 1443 • Newport News, VA 23601 • 757-596-5553

www.HelpHabitatforHumanity.org

CPSIA information can be obtained at www.ICGtesting.com
230322LV00009B/251/P

9 781600 378553